THE TAX-DEDUCTIBLE

Wedding

THE TAX-DEDUCTIBLE
Wedding

More Wedding and **Fun**, Less **Fret** and **Debt**

Sabrina Rivers

ILLUSTRATIONS BY NICOLE HOLLANDER

gpp
life

Guilford, Connecticut
An imprint of Globe Pequot Press

GPP Life gives women answers they can trust.

Copyright © 2010 by Sabrina Rivers

Illustrations © 2010 by Nicole Hollander

GPP Life is an imprint of Globe Pequot Press.

Text design: Sheryl P. Kober
Cover and interior illustrations by Nicole Hollander

Library of Congress Cataloging-in-Publication Data
Rivers, Sabrina.
  The tax-deductible wedding : more wedding and fun, less fret and debt / Sabrina Rivers ; illustrations by Nicole Hollander.
     p. cm.
  Includes index.
  ISBN 978-0-7627-5086-3
1. Weddings—Economic aspects—United States. 2. Weddings—United States—Planning. 3. United States—Social life and customs. I. Title.
  HQ745.R584 2010
  395.2'2—dc22

                                                      2009025341

Printed in the United States of America

10 9 8 7 6 5 4 3 2 1

Disclaimer: This book will provide you with many options to help you achieve your goal and still keep the fantasy. As with all advice, please consult your tax advisor as the tax laws requirement may slightly vary from state to state.

For Mom:

Words alone cannot express what you mean to me.

Thanks for cooking all those homemade meals, checking homework, encouraging good study habits, making sure I made it to school on time, and supporting events big and small.

Along the way you have been my best friend, therapist, teacher, and favorite travel buddy.

With all of that you continue to encourage me to seek my own path in life and to never forget to live in the moment.

I am grateful that you are my mom.

Contents

Introduction

Many women out there, myself included, have dreamt about our wedding day since we were little girls. We have fantasized that our special day will be a grand, flower-bedecked affair with lots of friends and family in attendance. We have thought of every detail, down to the last bit of tulle and silk ribbon. Most of us have visualized our wedding taking place in *the* perfect setting, whether that be a tropical beach, a villa in the Tuscan countryside, or a beautifully decorated hotel or restaurant. Sure, many of these ideas change as we get older and wiser, but our dreams never seem to go away. This pressure to wed is so ingrained in our psyche that before wedding bells even start ringing, we have tons of preconceived notions about what our wedding day should be like.

This pressure to wed is so ingrained in our psyche that before wedding bells even start ringing, we have tons of preconceived notions about what our wedding day should be like.

Combine the importance of this milestone in a woman's life with a tendency to be detail oriented and the desire to take care of everyone, and you can see why some women become completely absorbed by the planning process. We dive right in, and if we are not careful, the stress and worry of planning can take over our lives. It's precisely because we care about others and all of the little details that make the day so special that we fret over choosing just the right menu so that Aunt Maggie, who hates shellfish, will be happy; worry whether or not our best friends will look good in their bridesmaids' dresses; or want to make sure that we don't sit Cousin Louisa next to Cousin Jackie, who is now married to Louisa's ex-husband. All of this agonizing over things takes its toll and can drive some brides over the edge.

Weddings and the importance of marriage in a woman's life are things we can all relate to at some level. This universality unites women into a sisterhood that is wholly different from the way men interact with one another. As women, we naturally share intimate secrets and talk about our hopes, dreams, and lives, and this intimacy links us together as sisters, creating an unbreakable bond that can last a lifetime. No matter what part of the globe we hail from, weddings and the importance of marriage are common threads that many of us share. In our minds, everything must be flawless—the weather, the ceremony, the reception, you name it—and if things don't go off without a hitch, we are disappointed that the day wasn't a success.

There is a darker, more unpleasant side to this insistence on perfection, however. Many women (and a few men) have wedding issues, fixations, obsessions—call them what you will—that they have had since childhood. It's almost like a secret illness that no one wants to talk about. Blame it on *Cinderella* or *Snow White*—pick any fairy tale. I guarantee you that hiding somewhere in the story you will find preconceived notions about how life is only "happily ever after" if you get married. This Cinderella complex has made some women irrationally obsessed with their dream of the perfect wedding.

Think of it this way. *Cinderella* is a fairy tale told to little girls who don't understand the difference between myth and reality, but sometimes that can carry over into adulthood: The little girl inside each bride says that the wedding has to be just wonderful. It is what dreams are made of and what that little girl has been contemplating since she first heard stories about enchanted princesses who lived in castles and were rescued by handsome princes. These same story lines about love, relationships, and marriage even spilled over into play. In her world of make-believe, the little girl enacted pretend weddings with Barbie and Ken, and that is how her vision of weddings and marriage was formulated. The Mattel toy company, creator of our happy couple, tapped into this fixation on weddings by providing wedding gowns and veils for Barbie and tuxedos for Ken. These dolls defined womanhood, fashion, and marriage for little girls like few other cultural icons. The main difference between Barbie and Ken's wedding and the little girl's adult wedding was scope and scale: Barbie's wedding was only limited by the imagination of a child.

Unfortunately for caterers, wedding planners, parents, grooms, and anyone else associated with the bride, this same little girl is often still the one calling the shots when it comes time to plan the wedding. She may have grown up, but just talking about the wedding makes the little girl come out in a lot of women. It's as if the little girl has possessed the adult bride and taken over her personality. This can be scary when you realize that this little girl will be making decisions about how to pay for a wedding. When you consider how much the average couple spends on wedding festivities today, the last person you want calling the shots in money discussions is a child, and a petulant one at that.

This whole Cinderella-complex phenomenon has led to some out-of-control spending and over-the-top extravagances, for both the wedding ceremony and the reception. I wonder what Cinderella would say if she knew she had started a revolution when she married her handsome prince. Maybe it's this whole fairy-tale view of things and lack of restraint that has led to the badly behaved brides, but this out-of-control behavior has become so common that we now have a name for these crazed brides—Bridezillas. You know who these women are; in fact, you may even be one yourself. They are the spoiled, impossible brides who still think that they are planning a wedding fit for a princess. And believe me, they expect to be treated like princesses, too, no matter how small the price tag or guest list. They don't care how much anything costs or what kind of effort it takes to pull off the wedding as long as it is done the way they want. They are going to get a perfect wedding, reality be damned. The problem with this no-holds-barred attitude toward the cost of the wedding is that not everyone can spend a princely sum on his or her wedding—and it's this very lack of financial discipline that has led to weddings being bigger than a bride's purse.

Wedding Bells and Dollar Signs

Don't misunderstand my intentions; I'm not trying to change the world, and I certainly wouldn't want to be accused of crushing anybody's dreams.

There is nothing wrong with big, over-the-top, extravagant weddings—if you can afford them. I'm just pointing out that while a wedding may be romantic and filled with flowers, there is a more serious side to pulling one off. If you skim through glossy wedding photos or play a part in a wedding, at some point you will begin to ask yourself some of the same questions I have (and that most people would ask, too, if they weren't so afraid of having their heads chopped off by a ballistic bride): "How much did they pay for all of this?" "Who decided on those hideous bridesmaids' dresses?" "I wonder if that handsome best man is single? Maybe if I play my cards right, I'll get to meet him." "Thank god I don't have to wear that yellow taffeta."

All kidding aside though, wedding finances can be steep, and if you're not careful, they can put a huge strain on your pocketbook and your relationship—even before you tie the knot! But don't worry. I'm here to show you how to get around these obstacles and get the most for your hard-earned money. I'll show you how to achieve wedding-day bliss without going broke and include some tips on how to save money on your honeymoon, too. Throughout this book I will provide you with information on how to:

- Save money on your wedding and honeymoon

- Find alternative planning options that are practical and economical

- Find the tools you need to maintain control over the wedding-planning process

- Keep yourself organized, focused, and on task

- Weave through the maze of wedding vendors and find the best for the money

- Cope with all the wedding stressors—the wedding itself, your wedding party, and your relatives

So how do you learn to successfully manage the financing of your wedding? Are there books, guides, Web sites, or classes you can take? Where do you start? Most wedding guides don't really address the financial realities involved in planning a wedding and almost never discuss what the financial repercussions will be once the wedding is over. How much financial planning you do before your wedding and the amount of fiscal discipline you exert throughout the entire process can make a big difference on how your finances look after the glow of the wedding wears off. Sadly, too many couples saddle themselves with large financial burdens in order to pay for their dream wedding because they lose sight of the bottom line. It's easy to let the budget get away from you, so much so that some couples find that after they say "I do," wedded bliss often turns into marital blues.

Examining the statistics for the wedding industry, the *Washington Post* reported in an August 9, 2005, article that the average bride is twenty-seven years old, her groom is twenty-nine, and their engagement lasts around seventeen months. The article continued by citing that over forty thousand weddings occur annually with an average cost of $26,327. The article also pointed out that in metropolitan areas, this number can be as much $10,000 higher due to the much higher cost of living. When it comes to actually paying the tab for the wedding, few parents nowadays pay for the whole thing—only 25 percent. The days of dreamy wedding plans like in the classic movie *Father of the Bride* are long gone. Compare that to just 27 percent of the couples out there who pay for the entire wedding, and you can see that there are quite a few couples who need help filling the substantial gap in the funding of weddings.

When it comes to actually paying the tab for the wedding, few parents nowadays pay for the whole thing— only 25 percent.

So how are other couples managing to cover the costs of their wedding? They are doing a host of things, ranging from paying for some costs out of pocket, dipping into savings, liquidating 401(k) accounts, getting loans, putting the expenses on credit cards, and getting the remaining portion from their parents. The bad news is that almost half of all the couples surveyed said that they spent more on their wedding than they originally planned or budgeted for. In addition, a significant number of couples said that they ended up going into long-term debt just to finance the wedding.

The reason these couples go into debt in the first place is because weddings with all the trimmings, whether they are small, intimate affairs or not, cost a lot of money. The wedding industry is big business, and the costs add up quickly. The number of weddings has remained pretty steady, but according to a recent survey conducted by the Fairchild Bridal Group, the amount spent on ceremonies, receptions, honeymoons, gifts, and every bridal product or service continues to increase—$125 billion on 2.1 million weddings in 2005. Broken down, that comes to 40,400 weddings every weekend, with eighteen million bridesmaids and groomsmen, and 295 million guests.

Hand-Holding Advice—All the Way down the Aisle

The Tax-Deductible Wedding is here to help take the mystery and anxiety out of financing for your wedding. This book is your wedding-cost-control survival guide and provides practical advice on how to throw your dream wedding while saving money and having much of the cost be tax deductible. For example, most people aren't aware that a wedding or reception held at a museum or nature preserve that is also a 501(c)(3) nonprofit may be partially or entirely tax deductible. (It all depends on whether or not the rental fee for the space is tax deductible and if any portion of the reception costs related to food and service is tax deductible as well.) You also might not be aware that you can get much, if not all, of your wedding paid for by seeking out sponsors, a la Star Jones's wedding. She famously got most of her high-end wedding for free by soliciting big-name sponsors to cover the costs of everything from the invitations to the tuxedos for the groom and groomsmen, bridesmaids' gowns, airfare, and much more.

Not to worry; you don't have to be a celebrity to get sponsors. All sorts of brides and grooms are getting sponsorship to cover wedding costs. In fact, there are Web sites devoted to helping anyone find sponsors for nonprofit fund-raising events, sports events, school programs, and, yes, weddings. On the face of it, it might not be readily apparent what the benefits are to the business, but sponsorship can actually be a great opportunity for any

Linda and Louis's Wedding Brought to you by Ed's Fine Liquor and Champagne business, large or small. For starters, businesses get their name exposed to a large group of people in one shot and at a fraction of the cost of advertising in print and other media. In addition, by signing up to sponsor a wedding, merchants also get the opportunity to lend their name to a couple's wedding and thus be associated in consumers' minds with a happy occasion. This kind of name recognition and goodwill can't easily be bought, or at least not cheaply.

In this book, you will learn where you can go to find sponsors, how to work with them to offset some or maybe all of your wedding's costs, and how to barter with vendors and other providers to get services for your wedding for free or for a significantly discounted price. This book not only talks about the how-to of planning a tax-deductible wedding; it guides you through the process. So, dream on ladies and gentlemen. You will soon find out that your fabulous dream wedding is not only attainable—it can be had for a fraction of the cost you would normally expect to pay. For your buck, *The Tax-Deductible Wedding* guarantees more wedding, more fun, and a lot less day-after debt.

Chapter 1

The Cost of Today's Weddings

The wedding industry generates $70 billion a year in revenue. Now that's a whole lot of cake—uh, cash! In the past, the wedding business had been pretty much recession proof, but the economic downturn in 2009 had a direct impact on the cost and size of weddings that year. According to *The Wedding Report,* in 2009 "spending will be down 10 percent over 2008, which is already seeing a decline of 20 to 30 percent. In 2009, we estimate the average wedding cost to be between $21,000 and $25,000." It's already apparent that people are scaling down some parts of their weddings or delaying them entirely because of the recession. Many think that this downturn in the scope of weddings is just a reflection of the country's more sober economic mood. In fact, in 2009 the desire to save money and not appear insensitive to the impact of the bad economy has led to some interesting wedding trends. According to *The Wedding Report,* some of these trends include:

- Using free Internet alternatives for invitations and RSVPs, such as Evite.com, EZtoCreate.com, and MyPunchbowl.com

- Throwing smaller weddings with fewer guests

- Having weddings closer to home instead of exotic destination weddings

- Relying more on the help of family and friends and less on the services of professional wedding planners

- Emphasizing green/ecofriendly products and services

- Having less-ostentatious floral displays, centerpieces, decorations, and invitations (if traditional invitations are used)

- Having receptions that feature buffets or cocktails with heavy hors d'oeuvres rather than expensive, sit-down-dinner affairs

- Saving on the wedding gown by getting last year's designs; getting the dress from a discount house or during specials like Filene's famous "running of the brides" free-for-all; shopping at places that rent wedding gowns, such as www.bridecoutoure.com; or buying a used dress from a place like BravoBride.com

- Choosing smaller cakes paired with a groom's cake or less-traditional desserts such as cheesecakes, miniature cakes, and cupcakes instead of the traditional multitiered cake

- Saving on the cost of venue rentals and other services by not booking during peak hours and seasons

- Choosing all-inclusive packages rather than using multiple vendors

Depending on how long the recession lasts, only time will tell if these trends are permanent or if they are just a temporary blip on the screen. The wedding industry has historically seen increases over time, and this is still one area where parents, brides, and even grooms are reluctant to scale down on spending.

A Bridal Breakdown (Of Numbers, of Course)

According to the Condé Nast Bridal Group, publishers of the magazines *Brides, Modern Bride,* and *Elegant Bride,* a survey conducted by Global Strategy Group (2007) found that 59 percent of couples contribute to their weddings and 30 percent of couples self-finance their weddings. Of that 30 percent:

- 66 percent use their savings

- 49 percent use their credit cards (of which 36 percent are existing credit cards and 13 percent are newly opened credit cards)

- 17 percent take a second job

- 10 percent take out loans

One in three brides—32 percent—will spend more money on their wedding festivities than they originally budgeted for. Why? With all the stress of juggling work schedules and planning for their wedding day, it's common for anxious brides to be so wrapped up in preparing for the festivities that they lose track of the costs. It's easy to get lost in the nuptial-planning frenzy that includes shopping for the bridal gown, meeting with caterers and wedding planners, finding a venue, choosing colors and flowers, getting invitations printed and mailed, and dealing with friends and family.

There are also family pressures to hold a certain size or style of wedding, and brides often feel pressured to invite more people than they originally planned. The number of guests is one of the biggest reasons wedding costs skyrocket. And let's face it, we have become a country of image-obsessed people who want to feel important or have the same kind of over-the-top wedding as some rich celebrity. It's also not uncommon for parents to pressure brides about their weddings and push them to have big, elaborate affairs because they want to prove something to their friends or relatives. Even the best-intentioned bride can lose control of her budget and spending.

Often, it's only after the wedding and honeymoon—when the bills start coming in—that the real cost of the wedding is apparent. By then it's too late to do anything, and many hapless couples are forced to come to grips with the financial cost of the wedding. This sticker shock can be a real eye-opener for some, especially those whose profligate spending led them to overindulge their whims. These couples fell short of their budget goals and didn't pay attention to where they spent their money—or how much. Now they have to find a way to pay for their lack of discipline.

When it comes to spending on your wedding, the only way to truly know what you're getting yourself into is to keep very close tabs on your budget every step of the way. You can't let your emotions take over, or your spending will run amok. If you lose sight of the big picture (which, hello, is married life, remember? The stuff that comes after the big day?), you will end up drowning in debt. Any financial expert, wedding consultant, or intelligent person will tell you that you don't want to start your new life together as a couple wallowing in debt. Fighting over money is one of the leading causes of stress in a marriage and a leading cause of divorce.

"Okay," you may be asking yourself, "I know there are pressures, but what is it that couples are or aren't doing that lets things get so out of control?" "How can flowers be so expensive?" "I don't understand what it is that brides and grooms are doing that makes a wedding cost so much?"

The reasons are actually pretty simple. It goes back to simple math and keeping track of the numbers. In general, wedding costs get out of hand due to a lack of budget planning, a lack of understanding of the real costs of products and services, not reading the fine print in contracts, and a lack of financial fortitude. Basically, couples aren't keeping detailed records about where they are spending their money, they aren't keeping track of receipts, and they aren't sticking to their budget because they are letting their emotions dictate their money decisions. All of this happens when couples:

- Don't agree in advance what their budget priorities are

- Don't have a realistic, itemized budget and stick to it

- Don't take into consideration incidental fees, like tips, which can be a hidden cost

- Get so caught up in the plans that they don't organize their spending and bill paying

- Don't keep good records of receipts and what payments and fees are due and when

- Don't plan for unexpected fees

- Lose sight of what is important (the world isn't going to come to an end if the napkins are teal instead of seafoam green)

- Are overcome by the pressures of having a perfect day and trying to live up to everyone's expectations

How to Avoid Wedding-Planning Anxiety

What was the first thing you did after you were engaged? More than likely, you told everyone you knew about your happy news, and in your excitement you probably even told a few strangers. Chances are you bought a bridal magazine, too, or you went online and started researching everything you could that pertained to weddings. You looked at things like where to get the best dresses and tuxedos, who offered the best entertainment, which caterers had the best food, and so on. It's okay to be enthusiastic—this is an important milestone in your life. Did you find, however, that the more you researched weddings, the more the sheer scope of the project began to overwhelm you? Did a sneaking sense of panic begin to set in? If so, don't be alarmed; that's a perfectly normal response to getting engaged. With wedding advertisements everywhere you look, it's easy to be bombarded by information and start to feel a little beleaguered.

If You Are Humming Billy Joel's song "Pressure," STOP

Even the most organized brides can get lost in the maze of decisions about venues, seating arrangements, catering menus, wedding cake choices, gown selections and fittings, and so on. It can be pretty hard to decide which direction you should take to get started with your wedding planning. Wedding marketers will tell you what style of wedding dress is appropriate to the season, the formality of the ceremony, and so on, and you may feel pressured to have a certain type of wedding because some celebrity did things a certain way, but only you can judge what will make you comfortable and how you want people to feel when they attend your wedding.

By doing your research before you begin planning, you can keep your head when you are bombarded by others' opinions. Don't succumb to the wedding noise in your head and stay calm. You may be tempted to wear a certain style of dress in response to the voice of your mother droning on in your head, but you have to learn to tune these voices out and make up your own mind.

Remember our earlier discussion about knowing every detail of your dream wedding since you were a little girl? Well, here is one instance when that kind of obsession with detail can help alleviate anxiety—not increase it. You already know what you want, but you just need to be aware that there will be lots of pressure from friends, relatives, wedding planners, merchants, you name it, and they all will tell you that they know what is best for you. You don't have to give in to what other people want. Stick to your guns. Do what makes you comfortable; the objective is to eliminate or reduce stress, not add to it. You can't be at ease about any of the decisions you are making if you feel pulled in different directions.

Many of the things you will have to make decisions about can be fraught with underlying emotional baggage or tension, and this can cause friction between you and your family and friends. Hopefully you and your spouse-to-be will support each other no matter what. This will be a test of your devotion and dedication to each other. It is not the time to close ranks or take sides over silly things like seating arrangements and menu selections, however. Some of the things you will have to consider include:

- Do you know what type of wedding you will have?

- How much do you want to spend on your wedding?

- How will you pay for your wedding?

- Will you have a formal sit-down dinner or something more casual?

- How many people are attending the ceremony? How many will attend the reception?

- What type of food will be served?

- Will you have a groom's cake?

- Will it be an open bar or a cash bar?

- How many bridesmaids and groomsmen will you have?

- Will you hire a professional wedding consultant?

- What is your color scheme?

- Where you will be registered?

- What is your china pattern?

This list is by no means comprehensive, but it does give you an idea of the kinds of decisions you will have to make on a daily basis until the planning process is completed. The only way to keep your sanity in the face of all these details is to stay focused on the big picture. It's not going to be the end of the world if you can't have the historic church on the water for your ceremony, and the planet won't stop turning on its axis if your mother disagrees with your color scheme. Just remember that you are marrying a great guy and that the wedding is a celebration of your love for each other with the people who mean the most to you. This is a happy occasion!

Free Ideas for Weddings

So where do you start? Wherever you go, bookstores and newsstands seem filled with wedding magazines that range from regional, local magazines to destination weddings—and that is just the tip of the iceberg. But don't rush out to buy the latest very thick, very expensive bridal magazine; instead check to see if your local library has them. That way you can find out which magazines speak to your sense of style, values, and budget, and then you can go out and buy only the ones you need.

The following are other ways you can easily get ideas for your wedding that don't cost anything but time and maybe some gas in your tank:

- Visit bridal shops or bridal departments at department stores like Macy's, Lord & Taylor, JCPenney, Kohl's, Dillard's, Macy's, Bloomingdale's, and so on

- Talk to your mom, your friends, and other family members about their weddings; they will probably have lots of helpful ideas

- Watch bride, design, and event-planning television programs

- Look to your family's cultural background for ideas that could be incorporated in your wedding

- Look at wedding Web sites and blogs

If you want some fun and even zany ideas, television can be a huge resource. Two popular programs on the Style Network are *Whose Wedding Is It Anyway?* a show about how to plan a wedding with the help of your friends and relatives supervised by the expertise of a professional consultant, and *Married Away,* a show that covers most everything you need to know to plan a destination wedding. Neither of these shows is as popular as the programs hosted by wedding gurus like Martha Stewart or shows that include celebrity planners or planners to the stars, however, and they

tend to get overshadowed by wedding-themed specials that air either before or during peak wedding season. Some of the popular specials that aired in 2009 included *The Art of Cakes II,* a show about every kind of wedding cake style and cake decoration imaginable, as well as *Gorgeous & Green,* yet another wedding installation from Martha Stewart, which highlighted the planning involved for her assistant's gorgeous, ecofriendly wedding. Also featured was *Fat Free Fiancés,* which followed two couples in their battle of the bulge in the months before their wedding, showing how they lost weight and how they did (or didn't) cope with the process and each other. Finally, there was *Most Outrageous Weddings,* which looked at the crazy, incredible weddings that people have had, like a ceremony that included jumping out of an airplane with the entire wedding party, bride and groom included, dressed in full formal wear.

Another source of wedding ideas is your own cultural heritage. America is a country of immigrants, and there are hundreds of different cultural traditions related to marriage. Finding out what the wedding customs of your family's ethnic roots are and then incorporating some of those customs into either your ceremony and/or your reception can be a touching gesture that is sure to be a hit with both families—and a unique and cost-effective one. Ask your parents, grandparents, and older aunts and uncles if they know about old family wedding traditions. Over time, families often create and develop their own symbolic customs that can make your wedding an expression of your distinct identity. If you need additional information, the Web site Life123.com has a relationships section with a wedding subcategory that lists wedding traditions by country, and you can also go to OurMarriage.com, which has information on wedding traditions from the past as well as from around the world.

In some African-American communities, brides and grooms incorporate the "jumping of the broom" ceremony into their traditional religious ceremony. Two Web sites in particular have useful information about incorporating this tradition into your wedding, African-Weddings.com and www.do-it-yourself-weddings.com. The latter shows you how to incorporate "jumping the broom" into your invitation.

Talking to people, getting bridal magazines from the library, and incorporating your family's heritage are all good places to get good ideas for free, but nothing beats the resources you can find online. On the Internet, you will find blogs and sites written for and by brides, grooms, consultants, caterers, designers, and more. These online resources can show you how to find the perfectly fitted dress, serve the right menu, and properly plan for, organize, host, and pay for your wedding day. One Web site, SuperWeddings.com, has an entire section devoted to unique, touching

The Tax-Deductible Wedding

ideas for the ceremony and reception and has suggestions that will make each guest, member of the wedding, and the groom feel loved, pampered, and appreciated. The following are just a few of the kinds of sites you could consider for more ideas:

- **Brides:** Bride.com, Brides.com

- **Grooms:** GroomsOnline.com, TheManRegistry.com

- **Wedding portals:** WeddingChannel.com, TheKnot.com

- **General wedding Web sites:** MarthaStewartWeddings.com, http://from-i-will-to-i-do.blogspot.com/

- **Wedding blogs:** Weddingbee.com, www.iloveweddings.blogspot.com

- **Honeymoons:** Lovetripper.com, www.honeymoons.about.com, www.thehoneymoon.com or www.honeymoons.com

- **Wedding cakes and food:** The Food Network Web site, www.food network.com, regularly features programs about wedding cakes, and in 2009, chef Michael Chiarello's show *Easy Entertaining* featured the food he cooked and served at his wedding (you can watch it online). If you have hours free to browse, just Google "cooking," "entertaining," or "weddings," which will yield thousands of sites with ideas about reception menus that you can prepare yourself or share with a caterer.

- **Wedding gowns:** Web sites of high-end wedding-gown designers like Vera Wang (www.verawangonweddings.com) and Monique Lhuillier (www.moniquelhuillier.com) are great for ideas about wedding-gown styles. Also check out the Web sites of couture designers who dabble in wedding gown design, such as Armani and Chanel. One of the best sites for couture wedding gowns is LuxuriousWedding.com.

- **Other sites:** HGTV's Web site, www.hgtv.com (that's Home and Garden Television to the uninitiated), has an entire category of shows, tips, and ideas related to weddings. Everything from party planning to wedding, decorating, and entertaining advice is covered on their shows.

Wedding trends and fashions come and go quickly, and you will find that what's hot now may be passé next year. Savvy brides keep up-to-date with what's new by watching wedding-related television programs and surfing bridal sites and blogs on the Internet. In addition to the ones already mentioned, in chapter 7 I include some great recommendations for other sites and include my top ten list of the best online resources to save you time, hassle, and, most importantly, money.

The Roller Coaster Ride

The wedding process is psychologically draining, despite the fact that it is a happy time in your life. Just the thought of walking down the aisle can create anxiety, and many times fears about commitment and making the right decision can cause a lot of stress. Among all the decisions to be made, the most important may not be what style of wedding it will be, but instead the costs that will be involved. How will you pay for the wedding of your dreams? Can you handle the stress of managing the budget and expenses?

As you go through the planning process, your emotions will be on a roller coaster ride that will affect every aspect of your relationship as a couple. And you're not alone. Thousands of other brides around the country are going through the same thing. During the planning you will be making hundreds if not thousands of consumer-driven decisions, and just like other consumers, your emotions, as well as the size of your pocketbook, will influence how much you spend and what you buy.

Unfortunately, each year the price for wedding-related goods and services goes up, and brides-to-be are bombarded by advertisers to purchase the latest hot wedding favor or use a certain service to make sure their wedding is totally hip. That is why it's so vital that you have some financial fortitude; otherwise, you could be seduced by images of wedding gowns, beautifully decorated tables lit by candlelight, diamond engagement rings, and flower-bedecked venues. If you aren't careful about managing your time, money, and stress, your wedding planning could cause a psychologi-

cal meltdown. If you let your emotions get the best of you and insist on perfection, you could jeopardize your ability to make sound decisions. In this
volatile atmosphere, you run the risk of jeopardizing your financial health,
your mental health, and your relationship with your soon-to-be spouse.

STOP. THINK. PLAN. You don't have to succumb to the madness; you
can do this. You can exhale now. Everything will be fine as long as you realize that despite all of the romance and the roses,
weddings are big business. Vendors are in business to make a profit. Once you accept this, you
shouldn't be tempted by everything you see, hear,
or read. Keep your head on your shoulders and
don't forget your priorities. Remember who you
are and why you fell so madly in love with your
partner in the first place. The ultimate goal of the
wedding is to celebrate your love and honor your
new beginning as a couple—not to see who can
throw the most expensive or elaborate wedding for three hundred of their
closest friends. Keep your values close to your heart, and no matter what
kind of wedding you have, you can take comfort in the fact that you will
have the most gorgeous, heartfelt, and stress-free (tax-deductible!) wedding
imaginable.

> *Everything will be fine as long as you realize that despite all of the romance and the roses, weddings are big business. Vendors are in business to make a profit.*

Determining What Style of Wedding You Prefer

In order to know how much your wedding is going to cost, you will have to
know what style of wedding you envision. This is essential, because the style
(type of ceremony, number of guests, level of formality, type of reception)
impacts how much work is involved in the planning process, the amount
of time you need to plan, and the costs. If you haven't been planning your
wedding since you were a little girl and have no idea what kind of wedding
to have, the following is a technique that decorators use when a client is
unsure about what decorating style or color scheme they like. The benefit
is that it helps the client discover for himself or herself what style they
respond to most viscerally.

traditional Bouquet.

↓ wedding tiara with LOCAL Fruit

sams

Bouquet with cats.

Here's how to do it. With your groom, go through all the wedding magazines that you have and tear out the pages that have a look, style, fashion, or approach that each of you really loves. (Please only do this with magazines that you have purchased; never do this with magazines from the library.) Don't think about the picture a lot; just let your first impression tell you what you like. You can figure out why later. Label your choices as "his" and "hers" and in order of preference so that you have first-, second-, and third-choice piles.

Get a three-ring binder, some clear plastic sleeves, page dividers, and sticky-note pads from an office supply center, and label the divider tabs by categories such as wedding gown, bridesmaids' dresses, groom's and groomsmen's attire, reception ideas/styles, floral designs, musicians, caterers, wedding hairdos, reception favors, and so on. Put the torn-out sheets into the plastic sleeves by preference, and then go back and evaluate what it was in each picture that made you respond strongly. Attach notes about why you chose each page and include ideas you might have for incorporating what you found into your own wedding plans.

Now that you have created a prewedding portfolio, you will have a better idea of which colors, styles, and ideas you prefer. As you flip through the pages, you will see a style begin to emerge as certain colors, textures, levels of formality, and other design elements appear more frequently. This will help you decide if you want a more elaborate, formal wedding or one with just a few close friends and family in the garden at your parents' house. To give you an idea of what other brides have done, here is a breakdown, at the national level, of the styles of weddings planned in the United States in 2008:

Traditional: 51 percent
Casual: 19 percent
Formal: 13 percent
Unique: 10 percent
Extravagant: 2 percent
Theme: 3 percent
Other: 2 percent

Now you and your groom need to have a meeting of the minds and figure out what style you want and where you fall in the chart. To quickly get a rough estimate of what your style of wedding will cost as part of the budget, you can begin the process of finding which vendors sell the products and services that match your style choices and how much each product or service costs in your area. When you do your research or meet with vendors, your style portfolio will be a helpful reference, and it will help the vendors determine what kinds of products will appeal to you. It might not seem like much now, but the wedding vendors will appreciate that you have put together a collection of your ideas. This will make their job much easier, and they will be able to give you exactly what you want.

The Mom-and-Pop Marketplace

The marketplace is filled with thousands of vendors all vying for your business. Unlike other industries, such as the automobile or banking industry, the wedding industry just doesn't have Fortune 500 companies dominating the marketplace; most companies are mom-and-pop operations or medium-size businesses. There are a few superstars within the industry, such as Martha Stewart and Vera Wang, but more often than not, your wedding vendor is a small operation offering a very specialized product or service.

So how do you find them? Most people in the wedding business get their customers through word of mouth and bridal shows, which is important to keep in mind when you are shopping around. In order to make an informed decision, get recommendations from friends, relatives, coworkers—anyone you can think of—before you blindly go out in search of anything. Find out as much as you can about how other brides have planned their weddings. Learn where they got their vendors from and how they found them. Ask a lot of questions at bridal shops, visit Internet portals and directories that offer lists of wedding-related Web sites, and read everything you can get your hands on about how much things should cost. According to *The Wedding Report,* here is a breakdown of where brides in the United States got their vendor recommendations and information from in 2008:

Family and friends: 86 percent
Internet sources: 84 percent
Bridal magazines: 66 percent
Wedding-planning books: 47 percent
Bridal shows or fairs: 36 percent

Tried and True Recommendations from Those You Love

When it comes to finding any kind of service or product, nothing is better than a recommendation from someone who has used it. That is why so many brides and grooms find their vendors by asking for referrals from friends and family. It's not just that you can get a testimonial from someone who knows the product or service—it's also the fact that these are people you trust. They don't have anything to gain by recommending, or not, whom you use to cater your wedding, who sews your dress, who is your DJ, or who bakes your wedding cake. This kind of reliability can't be stressed enough, because knowing that you are getting a reputable, trustworthy professional to handle any part of your wedding can take a lot of worry off your mind. And anything that you can do to reduce stress is always a bonus.

The Internet

It's hard to imagine now how we ever accomplished anything before the Internet arrived on the scene, but online resources are invaluable to busy brides, grooms, wedding planners, and anyone else involved with weddings. Not only can you buy a wedding dress, rings, and wedding favors online, but you can also track and calculate every aspect of planning and organizing the big day, from budgets to time lines and checklists. There are also sites that will let you build your own free Web site that can showcase photos, gift registries, and more. (Of course you need a Web site, because you wouldn't want to exclude the rest of the world from your joy.) These sites can also be helpful networking tools, helping to connect brides with other brides who are experiencing some of the same anxiety. (You'll learn more about all of this in chapter 7.)

Bridal Magazines

As mentioned previously, bridal magazines are another valuable tool in the busy bride's arsenal. These have been around for a long time and have the added benefit of being very portable, relatively inexpensive, and easy to find. They are also helpful because they offer new information every year, giving brides an idea of what is going on in the bridal fashion world, offering graphic illustrations that help brides define their look, and providing resources for finding vendors in your area.

Wedding-Planning Books

Just like magazines, books can be a great alternative to hiring a wedding planner for every step of your wedding design. Just like magazines, they give brides a chance to see just what things look like and can offer great advice. Unlike magazines, though, wedding books have about a two-year lag due to the length of time it takes to get a book written, printed, and into the marketplace. As a result, books should be only one resource of several.

Bridal Shows

Next we come to bridal shows, which aren't hard to find since there are six thousand held every year in the United States alone. They are so numerous that you can find them all over the country—the world, in fact. To find a bridal show in your area (or anywhere else for that matter), there are two online directories you can go to: Bridal Show Producers International (www.BSPIShows.com) and Association for Wedding Professionals International (www.AFWPI.com).

When you go to a bridal show, you will find the accoutrements of love and fantasy everywhere you turn, but don't be fooled by appearances: Vendors at these shows all have dollar signs in their eyes. They are there to sell you something, and it pays to have done your homework before you go and know exactly what you are looking for before you arrive. Prior to shopping and browsing the aisles, you should know what the going price is for various products and services in your regional market, be familiar with industry standards for negotiating contracts with vendors, and be able to recognize value when you see it. Each vendor will be highlighting his or her products, trying to persuade you that you are entitled to have anything you want. After all, it's your big day, right?

When you do go to a bridal show, make the most of your trip. Having so many vendors all under one roof can save you hours of time driving from one merchant to the next and lets you compare price, service, and quality among many competing suppliers at the same time. There is also the added benefit of being able to sample many of the food products on offer, so don't be afraid to take advantage of some freebies while getting some great ideas for your wedding.

Be sure to ask lots of questions, get brochures, and take the vendor list and map offered to you at the door. These will come in handy as you wind your way up and down the aisles, and they help you prioritize which vendors you want to see first. You can also jot down quick notes about who you spoke with and your impressions of their service or product.

Helpful Tips for Attending Bridal Shows

It is best to have a plan of action when going to bridal shows. It can be very overwhelming when you walk into a big convention center and see row after row of exhibitor booths all clamoring for your business. This is a great place to ask wedding vendors specific questions about your wedding and get their feedback about your plans, however. Ask about bridal-show discounts on the featured products and services that you might be interested in purchasing; often you can get deep discounts just by attending the show.

The following are some tips on how to make the most of a bridal show:

- **Buy advance tickets.** Try to purchase your entrance ticket online, because you can usually get discounts if you purchase in advance.

- **Make a plan.** Create a checklist of what products and services you want to find information about at the bridal show. (Some of the things you might want to include are wedding favors, wedding gowns, invitations, music and entertainment, tuxedos, caterers, gift registries, accessories, shoes, photographers, videographers, venues, and so on.) This will help you to collect the right information from each vendor. When you get there, take a moment to review the bridal brochure/directory before you start walking up and down the aisles. Target the places you most want/need to visit first, highlight those vendors, and number them according to priority. Try to go to as many booths as you can, and remember that you may not be able to get to all of them—bridal shows only last about four to six hours, so there won't be a lot of time for dillydallying. This is why you should see the most important ones first.

- **Bring some tools.** Bring pens, a small notebook for taking notes, some highlighters, and your business or personal card. Also bring preprinted mailing-address labels so you won't have to repeatedly write your name on countless information request cards. Lastly, bring a sturdy bag with you to carry all of the materials handed out by vendors. You will be loaded down with stuff, and the bags distributed at the show usually aren't sturdy enough to carry everything throughout the day. (After my second bridal show I learned my lesson and brought my own bag. I have a sturdy over-the-shoulder bag that provides me with much better support and is comfortable to carry. It also helps me move through the crowd more easily without hitting others.) Be sure to dress comfortably and wear sensible shoes. You'll be doing a lot of walking, so this isn't the time to show off your Jimmy Choos.

- **Bring some company.** Bring family members and friends (especially if they are bridesmaids) with you to the bridal show; it's nice to have other people with you that you can bounce ideas off during the day. Plus, they may have questions that you haven't thought of or considered. If the show lasts more than one day, you should go at least twice so you can check back with vendors that you may have more questions for. Also, bring your fiancé with you to at least one show so that you can get his opinion and he can ask questions. If you are going with a group, break up and go to different booths so you can cover more territory. Pick a time and place to meet up later, and take a cell phone with you so that you can find each other if someone gets lost. (Having a cell phone will also make it easier to let someone know that they should get to a certain booth right away if you find something that is a must-have or there is a special deal going on.) If you can't find your groom, you might find it hard to make a decision later about a product you saw if you both aren't together to hear the information the first time.

- **Take advantage of the freebies.** When you arrive at the show, be sure to take one of the complimentary wedding-planning books at the door, if one is offered. These are an invaluable tool for staying organized and can be used as a checklist of what you want to find deals on at the show. (If a wedding book isn't offered, get one of Martha Stewart's special *Wedding* magazines before you go, and bring the planning and organizing tear-out sheets that she includes every year. That way you can jot down your notes and comments about all of the products and services she includes in her workbook more quickly.) Also, don't forget to sample the food prepared by the bakers and caterers. (It's a good idea to have the groom with you, because you can save a ton of time regarding decision making about cake flavors.)

- **Check the discounts.** Make sure that the discounts offered aren't just good for the day of the show, which is common. Some bridal-show discounts can include a combination of services, such as a photographer and a DJ or extra nights at a resort, and these can mean big savings. If vendors don't advertise or offer discounts, ask; you may still get one. Don't forget to contact those vendors that you like for a follow-up meeting. If you're approached by an aggressive merchant, do not feel pressured to buy if you feel uncomfortable. Some reps can be very persistent, but stand your ground.

- **Enter to win the door prizes.** You never know what you might win.

Questions you should consider asking the vendors:

- How long have you been in business?

- Can you provide samples of your work at the show or by mail?

- Do you have a Web site that provides a color photo portfolio of your work?

- Do you have references that I can call?

- What is your payment policy, and when are deposits due?

- What is your cancellation policy?

- Do you provide a written contract?

- Do you have liability insurance?

- How many weddings do you perform a year? On an average weekend?

- Are you listed with the Better Business Bureau? (Make sure you do your own research; look them up on the BBB Web site, www.bbb .org, or call the BBB.)

Now that we have covered just how busy you will be trying to find out how much you think you are going to have to do, spend, think about, decide on, argue about, and stress over, let's get to the meat of the planning process and how to actually make your dream wedding seem less like a slow-moving train wreck and more like a well-orchestrated ballet. And that means learning some of the tricks of getting organized.

Chapter 2

Getting Organized and Managing Your Wedding

Ready, Set, Plan

You are now ready to begin your wedding-planning adventure in earnest. You may have started already by casually picking up a bridal magazine, but this is not going to be that simple. It is doable, however, if you stay focused, stick to your plan and budget, and don't let your emotions rule your decision making. Be forewarned: Before you know it, you will become completely absorbed in the process. There are many options to consider and decisions to make. At times it may seem like the more you plan, the more there is to do, and the more you do, the more your emotions are affected. The planning of your wedding could well be the most pressure-packed period in your entire life. All of the conflicting expectations from your parents, other family members, friends, and your soon-to-be family, combined with the financial demands, may make it feel like you are in a pressure cooker.

You may be anxious about your new role, whether you're a first-time wife or if this is your second time around. And you might be wondering what this huge life change will mean to your personal and professional life. You may also have doubts about your ability to actually pull this thing off; after all, a wedding is a huge event for anybody to plan, even when they have professional help.

Fortunately, I will guide you every step of the way and give you the tools, tips, techniques, and resources you will need to meet your goal. You

are lucky, because in this high-tech age of computers and the Internet, there are hundreds, if not thousands, of articles, Web sites, blogs, directories, and portals that provide tools 24/7 at the touch of a computer keyboard—and most of it is free! You can find all the tools you need to be well organized—heck, some brides have even found their grooms on the Internet, but that's another book. Many tools and documents can be copied into Microsoft Word documents and saved on your computer, or they can be downloaded to your computer so that you can edit and customize them. Now that many Web sites and blogs are optimized for mobile devices, you can even download everything to your PDA or cell phone so you can have your planning tools with you everywhere you go.

But let's not get ahead of ourselves here; we need to start at the beginning and get planning. Now that you are engaged, you must be ready to plan the biggest party of your life. Here are the top thirteen things you must do *first*:

1. **Relish the moment.** Take time to enjoy being engaged and share some private time alone with your fiancé, because once you announce your engagement, you won't have a moment's privacy until the wedding night and your honeymoon.

2. **Tell your parents.** Do this before you tell anyone, and preferably in person. If that is not possible, then an uninterrupted, private phone call will have to do. Once both sets of parents know, then you can tell your closest friends, especially if you want them to be members of the wedding party.

3. **Create a journal or memoir.** Years from now you will appreciate going back and reminiscing about your wedding day or sharing the experience with your son or daughter. A journal can be a precious keepsake that chronicles the vicissitudes of the wedding, and it can be a learning tool. Writing down your fears, concerns, joys, frustrations, and thoughts rather than just giving vent to your groom, and friends can also help diffuse tension and conflict. If you want to keep a journal of your thoughts, impressions, and

day-to-day activities (and if what you write about is fit for public consumption), then a blog is a great way to keep everything, including photos, in one place. There are many free sites where you can set one up in minutes (which I cover in chapter 7). Internet-savvy people who don't want to blog or already have a blog can create an online journal at LiveJournal.com. This is also free, but it is really a more traditional, private journal that just happens to be online. You can also purchase a traditional hardbound journal or a diary to memorialize your thoughts if you prefer putting pen to paper, and you can give a blank one to your groom as an engagement gift.

4. **Choose your wedding date.** Depending on the time of year and whether or not you will be getting married during the peak season, you may need more than a year to plan everything. A wedding during June, for example, could mean that you have to book your venue more than a year in advance, especially if it's a popular spot. The same goes for caterers, florists, honeymoon reservations, etc.

5. **Announce your engagement.** Now is the time to shout your intentions from the mountaintops, if you are so inclined, but most people just announce their engagement in the local papers.

6. **Decide on the style of your wedding.** I covered how to do this in chapter 1.

7. **Create a checklist that will be the template for your overall plan.** Sit down with the groom and make a list of all of the things that you think you will need to include and that will become part of your more detailed wedding book later. This process is just preliminary, but it can give you a clearer idea of all of the things you will need to plan from start to finish.

8. **Work with your groom to write your financial plan.** It is time to do the work of creating your budget and to determine how you

will fund your wedding. (Chapter 3 describes in more detail how to create a budget and get your finances in order.)

9. **Choose your bridesmaids and groomsmen.** You need to decide whom you want to help with the important tasks that are part of making the ceremony and reception successful.

10. **Choose your venue.** If your wedding is scheduled during peak season, you may have to do this the moment you choose your date. If you are getting married during off-season, venue availability usually is not an issue.

11. **Build your support team.** Unless you are Wonder Woman, you will have a hard time successfully pulling off planning your entire wedding. This is where the help of friends and family, and/or the services of a professional wedding consultant, can be a lifesaver.

12. **Create your wedding book.** Whether you choose to use a more conventional printed wedding book or create one online, it will become the single most important organizing and planning tool you have, and it will be useful to everyone involved in planning your wedding. Your groom can rely on it to keep up with what you both have chosen for every aspect of the wedding, and attendants can use it to complete their tasks. Vendors will like it because you will have your color scheme, ideas, and information right at your fingertips, and planners will love it because they can see what your vision is with just one glance. And family and friends will like it because they can get ideas for gifts, ways to help, and stay up-to-date with where you are in your checklist and time line. Details on what should be included in your wedding book are discussed later in the chapter.

13. **Choose your honeymoon destination.** The earlier you choose your honeymoon destination the better, especially if you are getting married during peak wedding and/or tourist seasons.

Depending on how luxurious or far away your honeymoon destination is, you will need a lot of lead time to get good rates on airline tickets and room reservations. Also, this will give you time to save enough money so that all of your money isn't just spent on the wedding. Chapter 5 lists some ideas for getting things for free or for significantly less money by getting your wedding and/or honeymoon sponsored or through bartering. You can also sign up for a honeymoon registry, such as Traveler's Joy (www.travelersjoy .com), which is free to join and gives your family, friends, and wedding guests the chance to help you cover the costs of your honeymoon.

Lists, Lists, and More Lists

If you are not a list-making person, this book and the wedding-planning process might just turn you into one. Creating and using lists is a common tool used by successful, organized people, and with all of the different tasks, time lines, and logistical details that you will need to manage, you will soon live and die by your lists. Here is the first of many lists yet to come—the bride's checklist (good groom's lists can be found at www.bridal-show.com or www.groomstand.com).

The Bride's Checklist

Twelve Months Before

- Discuss with fiancé what style of wedding you both want

- Discuss what level of participation you expect from your groom in the planning, and find out how much or how little he wants to do

- Compile your preplanning portfolio to help you discover what style of wedding appeals to you both

- Divide up the vendor research and assign tasks to each other, friends, family, and a consultant (if you choose to use a professional)

- Work with your fiancé to develop budget priorities

- Compile your budget worksheets

- Figure out what your overall estimated budget will be

- Depending on the wedding date (peak or off-season) decide on your ceremony and reception sites, and make reservations

- Create your time line

- Continue to research the cost of what you need to buy and/or rent

- Select attendants

- Discuss the guest list with your fiancé and both sets of parents, and decide on the final head count

- Hire the consultant, caterer, photographer, videographer, florist, musicians, etc.

- Talk about your honeymoon plans with your fiancé

Nine Months Before

- Shop for your dress, shoes, accessories, bridesmaids' dresses, and groom's and groomsmen's attire

- Register for china, linens, honeymoon, etc. with your fiancé

- Purchase your wedding rings

- Reserve the lodging for out-of-town guests (if your wedding is during peak season)

- Make honeymoon travel plans (if your wedding is during peak season)

Six Months Before

- Discuss the rehearsal dinner plans with your fiancé

- Work with a florist to choose your flowers

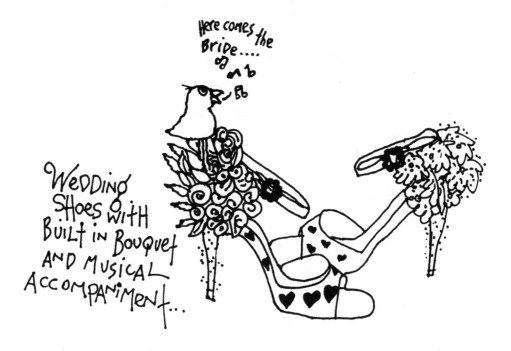

Here comes the Bride....

WEDDING SHOES WITH BUILT IN BOUQUET AND MUSICAL ACCOMPANIMENT...

- Place the order for printed invitations and announcements, and meet with the calligrapher if you are using one

- Mail announcements

- First dress fitting

- Select your officiant with your fiancé, and then meet with the officiant to discuss the ceremony

Four Months Before

- Confirm the delivery date of your wedding gown (if it is not already in hand)

- Reserve lodging for out-of-town guests (if your wedding is during off-season)

- Have your portraits taken

- Book the hairdresser and makeup artist

- Submit the shot list to the photographer and videographer, and give the musicians/DJ your musical selections

- Second dress fitting

- Shop for your trousseau

Four to Six Weeks Before

- Mail invitations

- Place announcement in local newspapers

- Call and get your belongings moved (if you'll be moving)

- Buy wedding gift for fiancé

- Buy thank-you gifts for attendants

- Plan bridesmaids' party and bachelor party

- Pick up your dress

- Write thank-you notes for gifts that you've already received

- Create a wedding day time table with your fiancé and wedding consultant (if using one)

Two Weeks Before

- Pack for your wedding day and honeymoon

- Send a reminder to your attendants about the dates and times of your rehearsal dinner and parties, and include a wedding day timetable

- Continue writing thank-you notes

- Confirm the lodging for out-of-town guests

One Week Before
- Get your marriage license

- Give the caterer your final head count

- Finalize your floral details

- Confirm the wedding cake delivery

- Throw your bridesmaids' and bachelor parties

The Wedding Book

The wedding book will contain your project management plan, worksheets, planning tools, goals, wedding design ideas, vendor and contact information, samples, swatches, photos, product information, and so on. It is your wedding compass and map, and it can help keep you on target, on budget, and on task. It is an essential reference tool when you feel tempted to overspend or can't remember what kind of flowers you wanted for your fall wedding. As I mentioned in chapter 1, Martha Stewart's annual *Wedding* issue has a tear-out worksheet included to help get you started.

Another print or hardbound option is to purchase a wedding organizer from www.exclusivelyweddings.com. They sell a line of products and organizing tools called the Organized Bride Collection, which has everything you will need to stay on top of things. Its wedding-planner kit includes a three-ring binder that comes with handles and closes up with a zipper like a self-contained briefcase. Inside are pockets and places to store swatches, notes, receipts, photos, and business cards, and the planner itself includes all the tools you'll need to stay organized, like worksheets, budget documents, checklists, calendars, and time lines. There are also handy tips and suggestions.

If you are more technologically inclined, you can find all of this and more online. One of the best sites, www.weddingwire.com, offers a very complete planning guide that's free, and most of what they offer can be printed out, too. Their tools are great because they keep every category of wedding planning in one place. They have thought of every aspect of organizing and planning, and they have the same tools for your groom. Their wedding book is what they call the Binder, which essentially becomes a customizable, interactive wedding book that lets you put vendor links and information into the Binder with just a click. As their Web site says, "Save paper and put your wedding binder online! Store links to Web sites you love, photos, wedding songs, as well as proposals and contracts from your selected vendors. All of your files are organized by category for easy recovery." If you want something less techie and more conventional, Amazon.com sells thousands of books that will help you with your wedding planning.

No matter what method or tool you use to create your wedding book, there are key areas of information and logistics that every book should always include. Here is my top ten list of what you will need to manage and include in your wedding book:

1. Budget and budget worksheets

2. Planning checklists and time lines

3. Wedding and financial consultants information

4. Wedding style and decoration ideas

5. Guest lists and invitations

6. Venue selection and seating arrangements

7. Wedding attire for bride, groom, attendants

8. Vendors and what to buy or rent

9. Food and drink (including the wedding cake and the groom's cake)

10. Honeymoon information

I can't very well go on and on about the importance of planning, budgeting, and using easy, available tools and not give the resource information you need, now can I? Although I cover financial planning and money management in depth in chapters 3 and 4, it makes sense to first discuss (as part of the planning process) one of the most vital aspects of wedding planning: budgeting.

How to Create a Budget

Mention the word *budget* to most people, and they cringe. Or they get the "deer in the headlights" look as if creating a budget involves some kind of voodoo magic, or that it's too hard to do. Think of a budget this way: It really is just a tool that you can use to track how your money is spent and to set goals and limits on how much you want to spend. The style of wedding (for example, a formal sit-down affair with open bar versus a casual buffet) and the number of guests are the two things that drive the cost of weddings upward, so from the beginning these need to be part of the decision-making process when plugging in amounts for venue rental, catering costs, invitations, and so on. When doing a budget, you need to make sure that you include all of the details related to the costs of goods and services that are part of your wedding. Here are the six steps to creating a wedding budget:

1. Decide on the style of wedding and number of guests

2. Determine all of the goods and services that you will need to buy/rent to host that style of wedding (including tips)

3. Decide on your budget priorities

4. Decide on the total budget amount, and also break it down by expense category (make sure you include as many details as possible when estimating your costs)

5. Decide on what expenses the bride or her parents will pay for and what the groom or his parents will pay for

6. Fill in your budget worksheet

Be a Financial Nancy Drew

Before you can even begin your wedding budget, however, you need to know where you stand financially in your life. In chapter 3 you will learn more about how to look at each other's spending patterns, see what your spending personality is, and see how you handle money intellectually and philosophically. This section, however, will help you understand how to assess you finances from a practical monetary standpoint. If you don't know how to figure out what your income and expenses are, no amount of analysis will do you any good. Don't misunderstand me—knowing the source of your issues with money is important, but not at this juncture. Right now the focus is on how to find the numbers you need to do the budget.

With that being said, here is the homework of the preliminary planning for putting together a budget. This stage is vital because I want you both to see where your money goes and how much is actually wasted on little things that you easily lose track of day in and day out. Each month there are probably a hundred little unimportant things you spend money on. The only way you will know just how much you are spending is to account for every dollar spent by looking at the totals for fixed expenses (those that don't change from month to month, like rent or a mortgage payment) and variable expenses (ones that change all the time, such as groceries, entertainment, clothing, etc.—these are the expenses that are the easiest to cut back on). If you can get a handle on both types of expenses, then you can better understand and estimate your current spending patterns.

For at least three months you should keep track of every dollar you spend. Be very deliberate and consider the reasons why you spent the money. Every time you buy something, pay a bill, or dispose of your money in any other way, make a note of what it is being spent on. Think critically about each dollar spent: Was it a required expense?

If you write a check for dry cleaning, pay a credit card bill, buy lunch, put gas in your car, or whatever, write it down on a piece of paper or put it in an Excel spreadsheet. Better yet, at the end of each day write down a list of every dime you spent and what the money was used for. Be sure to keep every receipt, no matter how small. Now you'll be able to see where your money is really going and if you are spending it wisely. Next, gather up all of your pay stubs, bank statements, renter's insurance bills, utility bills, auto and health insurance bills, receipts for the hair salon and dog groomer, and any other receipts or statements you have that show income and expenses. The amounts from this paperwork will be part of the information you'll need to complete your budget.

Start to think about what categories of income and expenses you and your groom have, and write them all down, considering what category each expense could go into. The following are some categories to consider and the expenses that they would include:

- **Home:** rent/mortgage, utilities, land line, cell phone, Internet connection

- **Daily living:** groceries, child care, dining out, dry cleaning, dog walking

- **Transportation:** gas, parking, insurance, repairs, public transportation

- **Entertainment:** movies, DVDs/CDs, plays/ballet/opera/concerts, monthly cable bill

- **Health:** insurance premium, health club dues, prescriptions, copays, over-the-counter drugs, vet bills/medications, life insurance

After three months you should have quite a stack of paperwork, of paycheck stubs, bank statements, receipts, and bills, as well as your lists of daily expenses. At this point you could continue to keep track on paper, but it is quicker and easier to download a free personal budget template to use in Excel. It is not hard to learn Excel, even if you aren't familiar with how it works. The beauty of using one of their spreadsheets is that they have already included many of the major income and expense categories, have laid out the budget by month for the year, and include built-in formulas to total columns. I recommend the free Personal Budget Worksheet template available at Microsoft's Web site, http://office.microsoft.com. Go to the templates section and type in "personal budget worksheet" in the search bar. This template will be great for your personal budget, but you can also get one preformatted for your wedding budget, too. Just go to the same search bar at the top of the page and type in "wedding budget." One should pop right up that you can download and edit to fit your needs. If you don't want to download your wedding budget, there are some great interactive online tools you can use, such as the wedding budget tool at www.wedalert .com/content/planning/budget.asp. If you are still unsure, WeddingDetails .com has a ton of great free wedding-planning checklists, worksheets, and articles right on their home page. Another great site for all things wedding-budget related is http://weddings.about.com/od/getorganized/a/wedding budget.htm.

Budget Priorities

Whether you are an expert at creating and using a budget or you are a newbie, before you fill out a worksheet or open an Excel spreadsheet, you need to discuss with your groom what your budget priorities are and why.

Our inability to openly and comfortably talk about money is one of the reasons there are conflicts about money in marriage. When you sit down to create a wedding budget together as a couple, this will be a litmus test of your ability to manage and negotiate money issues. It could be the first major financial discussion you have as a couple. Whether the two of you are paying for all of the wedding yourselves or are getting help from your parents, you both have to agree on what things are important and nonnegotiable, and what items are open to compromise.

When you sit down to create a wedding budget together as a couple, this will be a litmus test of your ability to manage and negotiate money issues.

This discussion will be different from the one you have with one or both sets of parents. If you are asking them for a large sum of money, it's essential that your budget priorities be clear and decided on in advance. You want them to know that you have dedicated time and effort to this part of the planning process and take this seriously. To alleviate anxiety and some of the tension involved in asking for money, it is best that you each approach your parents alone. If you were to do this together, your parents might not be as inclined to be as honest with you. No one likes to feel put on the spot, especially when it comes to money, so if you approach your family on your own, they might feel more comfortable about expressing themselves and discussing how much they are willing to contribute.

Here are the priorities that you and your groom must agree to when you begin the budget process:

- **The nonnegotiables.** These are the must-haves if you are to have your perfect wedding. For example, you have to have a June wedding, or he insists on having the wedding at his parents' country club.

- **The negotiables.** These are the things you can either eliminate or are willing to consider compromising on. For example, neither of you cares much about having tons of fresh flowers out of season, but you both want fabulous food, so a buffet rather than a sit-down dinner might be an option.

- **Budget-planning participation and responsibilities.** Both of you must be active participants in the budget-planning process and do the worksheets together. You must divide the responsibility for managing the budget and money and agree on the division of tasks and responsibilities, keeping each other updated on your progress and activities. You must keep detailed records of the money you have spent and save receipts for all your purchases.

- **Total cost.** You both have to agree about the total cost for the entire shebang, from the engagement to the wedding and the honeymoon, and you must stick to that figure.

- **Off-budget costs.** You must both agree that any large expenditure outside of the budget must be discussed, you both must agree to the expense or not, and if you agree to spend the money, the amount cannot exceed your ability to pay. You must agree not to go into debt for any reason and certainly never use credit cards.

- **Dealing with vendors.** Always get everything in writing, whether it's a return policy, cancellation policy, warrantee, or contract. Try to negotiate for a lower price whenever possible, especially with services that involve a contract.

Minding the Books

Now that you know what goes into a budget, it wasn't so scary was it? Okay, so now that you have done all of this, what's next? Since we have already discussed how to determine what style of wedding you want and you have decided on the number of guests, you should know by now how much money you'll have to spend. The next step is figure out how much everything costs so that you can fill in how much your estimated costs are in the appropriate column in your budget. That is why going to wedding and bridal Web sites, attending wedding shows, and visiting bridal shops to find out what you will need to buy/rent will be one of your more important tasks. This research process will get you the prices you need to do your budget worksheet. Because prices are influenced by geography, time of year, and other factors, this kind of primary source research can't be left to the last minute or be incomplete. Otherwise your worksheet and budget will not reflect the true expenses you will need to cover, and you will be doomed to go over budget.

The Tools

For those of you who are unsure of what goes into your wedding budget worksheet, here are the categories and subcategories of expenses that you will need to consider. This is not a comprehensive list, however, so you should try to think of everything you can when you sit down and do your budget so you don't get a nasty surprise later.

- **Ceremony:** location fee, officiant fee, marriage license, musicians' fees, ring pillows

- **Reception:** reception site, food, drinks, labor, valets, rentals (tents, glassware, china, heaters, etc.), cake, favors

- **Attire:** dress, headpiece/veil, undergarments and hosiery, shoes, accessories, jewelry, hair and makeup, groom's attire, shoes, cuff links, studs, suspenders

- **Rings:** his and her rings, engraving

- **Flowers:** ceremony, bride's bouquet, maid of honor and bridesmaids' bouquets, corsages and boutonnieres, flower girl basket, reception centerpieces, and miscellaneous decorations

- **Music:** ceremony and reception musicians/DJ, cocktail hour musicians, sound system rental

- **Photography:** photographer and videographer's fees, photo albums, additional prints, disposable cameras for candid shots

- **Transportation:** limousine or carriage transportation for wedding party, guest shuttle, and/or parking attendants

- **Stationery:** save the date cards, invitations, response cards, thank you notes, postage, calligraphy, guest book

- **Gifts:** for each other, bridesmaids and groomsmen, parents, welcome baskets for out-of-town guests

- **Murphy's Law:** a cushion for unexpected costs; about 10 percent of the overall budget

- **Tips:** Just as there are rules of etiquette about everything from the wording of invitations to who toasts the bride and groom, there are rules about tipping, too. See the next section for details

Tipping the Scales of Your Budget

When doing your budget worksheet, you want to be sure to include one of the most commonly overlooked costs that can take quite a bite out of your budget—tips. Most of the vendors that provide a service—such as waiters, bartenders, and chefs at the reception; limousine drivers; valets; photographers and videographers; hat and coat check staff; and musicians—

customarily get tips. Sometimes figuring out who gets paid and how much is simple because caterers and restaurants often include the gratuity charge on the bill, but sometimes it's not so easy.

Standard tipping amounts are dictated by your region and locale, but as an example, the following is a guide to who gets tipped and the range of amounts that are standard in the metropolitan Washington, D.C., area:

- **Valets.** If you were satisfied with the service provided by on-site staff such as valets, discuss with the company or person in charge of parking cars what to pay per car parked. Consider anywhere from a $1.00 per car and up. Make sure that the valets instruct the guests that valet service is complimentary.

- **Makeup artists and hair stylists.** For personal services such as makeup and hair styling, 15 to 25 percent is fair if you were happy with the service.

- **Limo drivers.** If your limousine driver or carriage driver was exceptional, 15 to 25 percent is a normal amount.

- **Coat-check staff.** They often get $1.00 per coat and/or hat.

- **DJs and musicians.** They should be rewarded if they played every song requested and kept the crowd happy. They usually get 15 to 25 percent.

- **Officiants.** Instead of making the faux pas of tipping the officiant, present him with a donation to the religious organization he represents if his is clergy. However, *do* tip a judge if you were married outside of the court (they can't accept payment while in their professional role at court, but they can do so off the premises).

- **Professional pastry chefs.** One person who is often overlooked is the professional pastry chef, who usually arrives with the cake, often finishes assembling and decorating the cake at the reception site (so that its easier to transport and can easily be repaired in case of

it's your wedding
Doo WAH, Do WAH
charging EVERYthing
Doo WAH, Do WAH
oN credit cards
oh yeAH,
yeAH
yeAH

a mishap), and decorates the table it will be displayed on. Her tip should be 20 to 25 percent of the cost of the cake, and don't forget to tip the driver if he also delivered fresh flowers for your cake.

Whether it is the DJ, the hair stylist, or the caterer, you should never tip if he or she is the owner of the company—but do tip the staff. Waiters, bartenders, and chefs often are tipped as part of the gratuity outlined in the catering contract, but if they did an exceptional job, a cash tip is a good idea (again, 20 to 25 percent). If you felt that your on-site coordinator, wedding consultant, or other event professionals were top-notch, they should be rewarded, too. A cash tip discreetly presented in an envelope is a nice touch for someone who went the extra mile.

If you don't want to have to remember the tips in the midst of your celebration, ask one of the members of your support team to be in charge of this.

The Consequences of Not Sticking to Your Budget

Americans tend to have some strange attitudes and complexes about money. On the one hand we feel perfectly comfortable opening up our private lives via Facebook and MySpace or on shows like *Oprah* or *Dr. Phil*, yet on the other hand we can't talk openly about money. As we have seen from the downfall of the economy in 2009, our inability to properly manage our finances (at the corporate level and personally) is the five-hundred-pound gorilla in the room. Even as children, we intuitively know that it's not acceptable to talk about money in public or even among family, and we see the repercussions in many places, especially in marriages.

Conflicts over money are one of the leading causes of divorce in this country. We used to be a nation of savers, and for generations we could reasonably expect that our children would do better financially than we did. That is no longer the case.

Aside from taking on mortgages that we couldn't possibly afford and living beyond our means, we have become overwhelmed by credit card debt—a condition borne out by the fact that many brides and grooms charge much or all of their wedding costs, knowing in advance that they can't afford to pay the tab. This situation has become so serious for all consumers that, according to a story written by Tim Westrich that was published on February 4, 2009, by the Center for American Progress (American Progress.org):

> It is often difficult for consumers to find information about when payments are due and to understand what actions will lead to a penalty. In fact, credit card companies dole out $18.1 billion in penalties to

*their customers each year. Moreover, many credit card penalties, such
as late payments, come with the additional burden of an increase in
the consumer's annual percent rate, or APR, to the penalty rate. This
penalty rate can reach as high as 25 to 29 percent. The average penalty
rate in 2008 was 16.9 percentage points higher than the average purchase APR, or standard APR. For a household that carries the average
amount of $10,678 in credit card debt, being repriced to the penalty
rate would result in an additional $1,800 in interest costs per year.*

The need for ways to save has become even more pressing. But no matter how good the economy is, every bride wants to save on their wedding.
That is why we have provided as many ways as possible to save on the costs.
This includes a wide range of strategies such as finding ways to get certain
parts of your wedding tax-deductible, avoiding accruing any debt to pay
for the wedding, scaling down the scope of the wedding, and doing some
things yourself. If you truly want to save money and not end up in debt
afterward then creating and sticking to a budget is one of the single most
important strategies.

Now you know how to create your budget, but don't begin to enter anything into the budget worksheet just yet. There is still some other homework
you need to do. In chapter 3 I will discuss how to address your underlying
financial attitudes and describe some coping mechanisms that will help you
deal with money in a more responsible and psychologically healthy way.

Chapter 3

For Love or Money

Getting Financially Hitched

As a single person, you were probably accustomed to buying whatever you wanted, whenever you wanted, however you wanted. But when you hitch your wagon to someone else in marriage, you need to think of yourself and your groom as "one," as a working team. You literally will share everything—financial benefits as well as blemishes. Your credit history now becomes his, and vice versa. Until you both sit down and have a heart-to-heart talk about your financial goals and priorities, and are honest with each other about your individual financial health and history, you should *not* even think about planning a wedding together. It's sad but true: Most couples are more tight-lipped about their attitudes about money than almost any other topic. If you and your groom-to-be are going to be able to successfully manage the financial side of planning your wedding, you should discover what each of your personal money-management approaches are.

Most couples are more tight-lipped about their attitudes about money than almost any other topic.

This may prove difficult for fiercely independent types, but these adjustments are needed to seal your union smoothly. This chapter will help you come to grips with the emotional and psychological aspects of being financially prepared to plan the big day.

Discovering Each Other's Money Strengths and Weaknesses

When it comes to the financial aspects of the wedding, nothing is more important than being realistic and honest about your expectations, agreeing on what your budget priorities are, developing a complete budget, and being fiscally responsible and respectful of each other's needs, priorities, values, and goals. The money decisions you make before your wedding can have long-term effects after you are married. I know it's hard to talk about debt, money, saving, and spending when you're already stressing about the wedding dress and what your guests will eat at the reception.

Indeed, worrying about money can be an emotional drain. Financial experts agree that far too many brides and grooms don't discuss finances before they get engaged and that there are certain things they must discuss before they ever walk down the aisle. The way that you and your groom discuss money and the rules and habits that you set up now will affect how you handle finances throughout the planning process and once you are married. If you both sit down now and seriously talk about your current financial status, you can save yourself money, conflict, and heartache, and you might just avoid the financial pitfalls that many couples fall prey to early on. No one wants to start out their married life thousands of dollars in debt because of one day's indulgence, do they? However, if you want to have "the money talk" and change the way you manage money and your attitudes toward it, you first have to understand where your issues with money come from.

Your Childhood and Money

Did you have an allowance as a child? If so, were you a spender or a saver? Now that you're an adult, are you a spender or saver? You don't have to be a financial guru to recognize that there is a correlation between your spending habits and feelings about money as a child and your perception of money as an adult. A simple thing like deciding how much to spend on flowers or who pays the bills can raise all sorts of emotional ghosts from the past. Society plays a role, too, in influencing how we view money. Depending on where you live, your religion, political ideology, or a host of other reasons, money can be perceived as defining or reflecting our roles as men and women. Often money means power or the lack of it, and it's tied to our feelings of self-worth. Knowing what kinds of emotional experiences you had with money as a child and how you handled money then can help you better understand how your spending habits developed in the first place.

If you are a spender, do you somehow use shopping or spending money as a way to compensate for feelings of inadequacy? Do you use shopping to make you feel better about yourself? If you are a saver, do you feel you were denied things that you should have had as a child? How were you first introduced to money? Was it a love/hate relationship? All of these attitudes and experiences with money impact how you handle money now.

Your Parents' Spending Patterns

Just as much—perhaps even more—as your childhood spending can influence you now, your parents' habits and fears can significantly impact your financial persona. What type of spending habits did your parents have when you were a kid, and what are their spending habits now? Without even knowing it, your parents may have influenced your attitudes about money and caused you to take on some of their anxieties. Case in point, if your grandparents lived during the Great Depression, this experience probably changed the way they felt about money.

Most people who lived during this difficult time in our country's history never felt truly secure afterward. Scores of people adopted a waste not, want not mentality or developed neurotic, almost obsessive attitudes toward hoarding or saving. These Depression-era survivors never fully recovered from the feeling of impending doom, and they felt compelled to save things just in case the bottom fell out of our economy again. This fear of spending money was often projected onto their children, the Baby Boomers who grew up to be all over the map financially.

The Baby Boomer generation reacted to their parents' thriftiness in myriad ways that were almost always extreme: They became hippies who refused to have anything to do with money and wanted to live off the land, they spent tons of money on material things as if to prove to the world that they were better than everyone else, or they were workaholics driven by greed to become multimillionaires, such as Michael Douglas's character in the 1980s-era movie *Wall Street.* Conspicuous consumption became the norm, but then the economic crisis of 2008–2009 hit. It remains to be seen how this latest crisis will affect future generations, but one thing is clear: Ingrained behaviors toward money can have serious, challenging consequences.

I count myself lucky that when I was growing up my mother gave me an excellent financial education and conveyed to me how emotionally damaging money failures can be. When I see others struggling with money issues today, I marvel at her foresight and ability to instill in me the skills and values that have kept me out of financial trouble. She taught me the proper way to pay bills and the basics of managing a checking account, and she also taught me the importance of being responsible and staying out of debt. One example still stands out in my mind. I received a utility bill that I didn't have the money for, and I wasn't sure what to do. My mother recommended that instead of ignoring it or paying it late, I should contact the utility company, explain my situation, and ask for an extension rather than receive a late charge. (Late charges can negatively impact your credit rating in the long run.) While I have made a few mistakes, I have never gotten into any kind of long-term negative situations with my finances. The financial foundation that she gave me helped prepare me to manage my own money as an adult and set me on the right track.

Unfortunately, a lot of people don't get the kind of financial education I did, and often they suffer the consequences when they become adults. They soon find out that without even a basic understanding of how to handle their money, their lives will be financially limited. Some learn from their mistakes and don't do any significant long-term damage to their credit and financial health, but not everyone is so lucky. There are large numbers of people whose past mistakes have severely limited their ability to move ahead. Missed or late payments and bad credit can prevent many people from buying a car, buying a house, getting a job, or being approved for any kind of credit.

How Men and Women Spend

No surprise here: Men and women have different spending behaviors and priorities. We are simply hardwired differently, though of course there are exceptions to every rule. In general, men seem to have a goal in mind when they shop. They want to get in and out of the store as quickly as possible (unless they are shopping for tools or stereos!). Women can go both ways, vacillating between goal-oriented shopping and just window shopping. There can be times when we wander through the stores only to realize hours later that we ended up buying much more than we intended. Women do shop differently in other ways, too; we tend to take the time to find bargains and comparison shop.

A lot of men don't have patience with this kind of time-consuming shopping marathon, and that is why your normally supportive fiancé may throw up his hands in desperation during the wedding planning. It will be almost painful for him to endure your hemming and hawing as you try to decide if blushing pink versus dusty rose is the perfect color to include in your color scheme. As a group, women tend to be power shoppers and go the distance, especially when we are shopping for an important event like a wedding. This single-minded focus has been a powerful revenue engine in the wedding industry and has helped drive up costs over the years. Our buying power as a group (meaning women, not just brides) is substantial. A recent study by Gallup shows that by the year 2010, women will account for 60 percent, or roughly $1 trillion, of this country's wealth. If we are going to be controlling that much personal wealth, then we'd better start managing it properly—sooner rather than later.

Think about your habits. Do you come to the marriage with financial and credit "baggage"? Will your past mistakes be a drain on both of your financial futures? Can you both make adjustments if necessary and work toward your goals together? Can you both become better fiscal partners? Well, you're about to find out, because now it's time to look at each other's financial health.

Your Fiancé's Spending Personality

As you get ready to marry this man and share his life, how much do you really know about him financially? Does he ever discuss money with you?

Do you know what his spending patterns are? Is he a spender or a saver? Does he pay his bills, or do his parents pay his bills for him? More importantly (for his credit rating—and yours), does he pay his bills on time?

You need to know about his spending habits so that you can get a handle on how good or bad his money-management skills are. What kinds of things has he purchased over the last six months? Is there a pattern to his spending (or overspending)? Is he a video-game junkie, or does he have to go to every home baseball game? Can he afford to pay for these extracurricular habits? If these are regular expenses, what other big bills does he have to pay on a regular basis? This kind of regular spending will have to be included as part of your monthly household bills and could prevent you both from having any discretionary funds left for large expenses such as a car or a house—or a wedding!

Let's not forget how men and women's brains process information about what's important; we prioritize how we spend money differently. He may like electronics, and you may not think they are important at all. On the other hand, you may want to have nice clothes for work and feel that spending a little on shoes every month is nonnegotiable, while he's not convinced that having a pair of black pumps, black sandals, black flats, and several other shoes in black is a necessity.

Your Spending Personality

Now is the time for you to be honest (with yourself and with him) about how you manage money. Are you a saver or a spender? Do you live from paycheck to paycheck because you overspend? What is your credit like—poor, good, or excellent? You need to come to grips with your true net worth, assess how much debt you owe, and determine whether you can afford the wedding you are dreaming of. Do you even know how much you spend per month on food, rent, utilities, clothing, and so on?

Survival of the Fittest

Marriage is like the financial merger of two companies, each coming to the table with its own strengths and weaknesses. Each has its own cash and debt, and if they are to succeed as one company after the merger, they must understand certain things about each other. The same is true in marriage. You and your fiancé may not share similar spending habits, but if the merger is to work, you must merge your spending/saving philosophies. It won't be easy. You will need to determine what each of your strengths and weaknesses are when it comes to managing money, and then you can decide whose skills match the tasks of paying bills, balancing the checkbook, researching how you invest your money, etc. You want to make sure that the division of labor is based on what you are good at and willing to be responsible for and try to avoid the pitfalls of falling into stereotypes. This can only be done once you have had "the money talk."

Marriage is like the financial merger of two companies, each coming to the table with its own strengths and weaknesses.

The Money Talk

This will not be an easy or comfortable exercise, but it should be done. The goal of the money talk is to find out how financially solvent you are and if you will be inheriting both good and bad debt. You should each be honest with each other about what you owe, to whom you owe money, and how much. Sit down together and make an itemized list of what debts you owe in detail. This should include everyone you owe money to, how much you owe them, how much you pay to them each month, when the debt will be paid off, the interest rate for each debt, and what your record is with them. Have you ever been late? If so, how often, and when?

Once you know how much debt you have, then you need to work out what you need to pay off immediately (the credit cards that have high interest rates are a good place to start). Come up with a schedule for how much to dedicate to each debt and when you want to have the debt paid off, and determine who will be responsible for tracking and managing this process. Make sure that you take into account how you will meet your other living expenses and how those bills will be handled and by whom. Will you share the bill-paying tasks, or is one of you more suited to this? How much money will you need to put away for the wedding? Where will that money come from?

Determine what your goals are as a couple and write them down. Start with short-term goals and work your way toward long-term goals such as buying a house, buying a car, etc. In the short term, say the next one to three months, determine how much you will need to pay regular bills and living expenses, and try to focus in on things that can be scaled down to save for the wedding. In the next three to six months, try to pay off as much debt as possible and decide which bills you will pay off together. Between six and twelve months, start planning for your wedding, a new house, a new car, or a vacation.

Everyone is different, and it doesn't matter how you decide to meet your financial obligations, as long as you do meet them. Other people don't have to agree with your methods. What might work for one person may not work for another. Determine if separate bank accounts or joint accounts will work for paying your bills as a couple, and consider creating a "slush fund" for other items so that you don't need to dip into the funds in your primary bank account. If you choose to have a slush fund, you should set some parameters so that you only use it when absolutely necessary. You both have to agree on what the slush fund can be used for, set limits on how much you can take out at any one time, and determine how much either one of you can spend without the other person weighing in on the decision.

The Dreaded Budget

As I stated in chapter 2, there is some emotional and psychological homework that you have to do before you can begin plugging in numbers into your budget. Was I right? Did you find that after the money talk there was more or less income than you thought? Was there more or less debt and expenses? Now that you have been brutally honest with each other, you may have to go back and add some categories and expenses to your budget, but that is to be expected. This is an ongoing process that you should begin to do monthly. It not only keeps you on track and lets you know where you really stand financially, it also helps keep you aware about how much you're really spending—and on what. So let's do the budget. This is actually going to be the easy part, because it is just a matter of entering the amounts and numbers you already got from doing the really ugly parts of the job first.

Now it's time to fill in that Personal Budget Worksheet template I told you about in chapter 2 (the one you can download for free from Microsoft's Web site). The beauty of this Excel template is that you can quickly learn how to change the formulas, add and subtract expense lines, and begin filling in the cells by income and expense category. This worksheet should mirror your current spending patterns and include every single expense. Don't try to lie or leave out something, because when the subtotals are added up, you will find that your budget doesn't properly reflect how much money you will ultimately have to spend on your wedding. Really try to include little things and fill in accurate amounts. If you don't see an expense category included in the template, such as your wedding, by all means, add it, because every dollar unaccounted for can mean financial hardship when you are doing the wedding budget.

Depending on your work style, you could either do your wedding budget at the same time you are doing your personal budget or not—it's all contingent on whether or not you already have realistic numbers to put into your wedding budget. What is important is to set your budget up by month for a year and to make sure that every expense gets accounted for, no matter how small. Your budget is only as good as the detail you put into it, and the source of that information will be the documentation (bills, receipts, etc.) that I told you to compile earlier. Now you can enter your income sources and amounts into the income portion of the budget and fill in the expense category amounts. Make sure you refer to the running totals of expenses you have been keeping daily, weekly, and monthly. Compare those expenses and the amount you spent to the receipts, bills, and bank and credit card statements. See if there are expenses on your credit card or bank statements that you don't have receipts or bills for, or, conversely, look at your statements to make sure you didn't leave out an expense or category. As you enter each amount, the Excel spreadsheet will automatically be totaling columns and cells, and you should begin to see where your money is going.

Hopefully when the spreadsheet totals the amount for income and expenses, you will not be surprised by the results. The last thing you want is to discover that your expenses exceed your income. If you are really watching what you spend and follow the saving techniques I outline in chapter 5, you just might have some money left over each month to put toward your wedding. If not, then the budget will show you where you can reduce spending and if you can eliminate some expenses entirely. For example, try to see how often you really watch some of the programs on your premium cable television stations. Do you really need to spend an extra $30 a month to watch a show once in a while? Eliminate two or more premium channels, and put that $30 into savings for your wedding. How much do you spend a week on buying lunch? Figure out how much you can save if you bring lunch instead. Let's say that you spend $8 a day on lunch, which comes to $2,080 for the year (this may be more or less depending on your geographical area), and let's be conservative and say that if you brought your lunch, the cost would be cut by 50 percent. That is still $1,040 you could be saving for your wedding.

If you aren't inclined to use Microsoft's Personal Budget Worksheet template, there's an even easier budget tool that does the math for you. The Wedding Budget Planner is available at GroomsOnline.com and is a no-brainer. Just remember, whatever method or tool you use, be as diligent with the wedding budget as you were with your personal budget. Don't overlook any expense, no matter how small, because things can add up quickly. (Take an item and multiply that by the number of guests, and you can see how quickly things add up.)

Once you finish your wedding budget, go to your personal budget and add a new category of expenses called "wedding." Take the total amount from your wedding budget and enter that amount in your personal budget. If you wish, you can include some of the wedding budget categories of expenses here just to keep an eye on where the wedding money is going. Once you have added your wedding budget amount, you need to figure out how you will manage your finances for both the short term, which includes the year leading up to your wedding, and the long term, which will be your future together as a couple. Once you decide where you want to be in, say, ten years, it would probably be a good idea to get some professional help with planning your investment strategies. That is where the services of a financial planner can be invaluable.

Finding Financial Advice

Now that you have had "the money talk," you may have discovered that some good advice from an advisor might help you plot how you reach your goals. Financial advisors can show you how to maximize your investments and assets and find ways to save money or invest it for the long term so that other goals can be achieved, like saving for your children's education. If you can't afford to hire an expensive financial advisor, find out if any of your friends, family, coworkers, or members of your church would be willing to give you some free advice. Also, check with your bank; often their investment services department offers free financial planning as part of their services to customers. Be creative—maybe you could approach a local reporter and get him to do a story about how to get free financial advice, having him follow you as you go through the process of finding someone.

If this financial advisor is also a CPA or an attorney, she may be able to advise you about what kinds of wedding expenses are tax deductible and how you can better manage the money you already make. She might be able to show you how to maximize the earning potential or value of some assets you already own. If you own a house, have a trust fund, have a high-paying job with growth potential, or could possibly inherit some money, a good financial planner can help you see the big picture and how to meet your short- and long-term goals. And they might just save you a lot of money in ways you hadn't thought of before.

What to Look for in a Financial Advisor

Nothing is better than word of mouth when getting a recommendation for this kind of professional. If you do get a recommendation, the following are some of the things that they will need to address or satisfy if you are to benefit from their services:

- Do they understand your goals and plans for the future?

- Can they create a clear, easy-to-understand plan for how to reach your goals?

- Is there plenty of opportunity for you to ask questions?

- Are the financial products they are recommending in line with your budget, goals, values, and money-management skills? (If you don't feel comfortable with their recommendations or want to do something differently, say so. Don't be afraid to say no to something.)

- Do they take time to educate you on the available products and services?

- Are they accessible and easy to reach so that you don't have to waste time tracking them down?

Credit and What It Really Means

When you had your money talk, you learned more about each other's credit history. Now you need to understand how your credit score can hurt or help you. Each of you should find out what your credit score is and determine if there are things you need to fix on your credit report. One of the best places to do this is *www.annualcreditreport.com.* You can access all three of your credit reports (and credit scores) from Trans Union, Equifax, and Experian through this site. As a consumer, you have the right to receive three free credit reports per year, and it's best to do all three bureaus at the same time since they can have different or conflicting information.

It is important to fix anything on your reports that is out of date, incorrect, or doesn't agree. AnnualCreditReport.com will provide you with reports from all three bureaus, and if you want to get a more in-depth education about your credit scores and what they can do for you, the Fair Isaac Corporation, also known as FICO, can give you some good advice at www.myfico.com. They have been producing FICO scores since the 1950s and are the go-to people for credit scores and information. That is why your credit score is often simply referred to as your FICO score. The score ranges from 300 to 850, and your credit score determines how much money lenders are willing to give you toward the purchase of a car or a house, as well as your credit limit on your credit cards. Your credit score can even impact your job search since many employers now do background and credit checks.

So how is your score calculated? There are several factors that are taken into consideration. One is the length of time you have been with your creditors. For example, if you have had a credit card for a couple years versus a couple of months, that can impact your score. If you have applied for and been turned down for one, two, or three or more credit cards, that can negatively impact your score. If you have had a lot of inquiries into your credit, that can be damaging. If you carry large balances on your revolving accounts and don't pay them off on time or go over your credit limit, it can be bad for your score. If you have a long history of credit, this allows lenders and others to evaluate your credit worthiness based on your record of payments (either on time, late, or delinquent). Some other aspects that play into your creditworthiness are how long you have lived at your residence, how long you have been at your job, and the kind, amount, and status of your revolving credit accounts. Each credit reporting agency or institution has mathematical equations and other secret formulas that they use to formulate your credit score.

Your Debt-to-Income Ratio

Another factor that creditors look at is your debt-to-income ratio, which is determined by how much you have coming in (gross income) and how much you have going out (after you pay your bills). The acceptable debt-to-income ratio depends on the benchmarks established by each lending institution.

The following is a breakdown of the levels of debt ratio, from good to bad:

36 percent or less: This is a healthy debt load for most people to carry.

37–42 percent: Not bad, but start paring debt down before you get in real trouble.

43–49 percent: Financial difficulties are probably imminent unless you take immediate action.

50 percent or more: Get professional help to aggressively reduce your debt.

(*Source:* Gerri Detweiler, author of *The Ultimate Credit Handbook.*)

Get a Handle on Old Debt Before You Go into More!

As I mentioned in "The Money Talk" section, I strongly advise that if you and/or your partner have large amounts of credit card debt or other loans, you should both actively work to pay them off (or come close to it) before you tie the knot. You don't want to have to pay a higher interest rate for your dream home or, worse, have it snatched out from under you because of bad credit. Because of the bottom falling out of the economy, banks are now scrutinizing debt ratios, credit scores, and spending habits much more closely. They are reluctant to risk the same fallout as before.

Managing your money is not a passive act.

The way you manage your debt, bills, income, and disposable income says something about how you will manage your wedding budget and your personal budget as a married couple. Managing your money is not a passive act; it involves day in and day out discipline, good record keeping, sticking to a budget and not overextending yourself, doing the right thing by paying your bills (in full and on time), and not getting into more debt. If you come up with a financial plan that includes ways to save, invest, and properly manage your money *and* stay on track, then you can probably find a way to at least pay for part of your wedding. Use one of the online financial calculators (debt management, investing, net worth, etc.) such as those found at BankRate.com to find out how much you need to pay on each of your debts to bring the amount down or pay them off. Remember, getting a hold of your financial goals now will save you agonizing fights about money later, and it helps in planning a financially sound wedding and future. Here is an action plan to get you going in the right direction:

1. Order your credit report and make sure the information is correct.

2. Correct any information that is inaccurate.

3. Gather all of your bills and separate them into two separate piles: one for your revolving accounts (e.g., credit cards) and one for installment payments (e.g., car, mortgage).

4. Take a good look at your at bills and credit card payments, and find out what interest rates you are paying on each debt every month. Does this give you pause? What is your reaction? Did you know how high or low the interest rates were that you were paying? Are you shocked at the bills your partner has accumulated? They are now your bills, too.

5. Take a moment to decompress.

6. Either print out a financial worksheet or use an interactive one online. You can find some for free at MyMoneyManagement .net and Credit.com, as well as WomensFinance.com. The latter offers numerous free budget, worksheet, and money-management tools, and some of the best include a worksheet to help you track your payments to creditors, balances, interest rates on each card, and so on; another credit-related worksheet that can tell you how close or far away from your credit limit you are on your cards; a list of what bills need to be paid and when; a worksheet to help you track your daily and monthly expenses so you can see where your money is really going; a monthly budget to help keep your expenses and income in line with your goals; and a wedding budget sheet that will show you how to track expenses, make sure you stay within your spending limits, and how the two align (or don't).

7. Enter the amounts of each payment and the total due on each card or debt onto the financial worksheet.

8. If you are more of a techie, you can plug all of the same numbers for income and expenses into BankRate.com's handy-dandy financial calculator instead of listing them on the worksheet. It will reveal your debt-to-income ratio, your highest interest rate

payments, which bills you can pay off before your wedding, and which ones you can pay after you are married. All of these worksheets and tools can also be useful when you sit down with a financial planner.

The Budget and Beyond

Now you can create your budget and plan. You can use accounting software like Quicken or QuickBooks to do your budget, or you can just create one in an Excel spreadsheet to get started. (As I mentioned before, there are Excel budget templates that you can download for free from Microsoft .com.) When you do the budget, be sure to estimate all of your expenses for the calendar year by determining how much will be coming in and out of your household. Create separate slush, emergency, and savings accounts. Establish an agreement concerning approval and veto processes for large purchases. If you must make purchases, look at alternatives that can save you money. (For example, if you need to buy a car, consider waiting until the end of the year. Around September and October new models usually replace the old, and you can get a good deal. This is true of appliances and other products as well.)

Review your financial goals every six to twelve months. Evaluating how well you are sticking to your budget, sooner rather than later, may help you correct any financial issues before they get out of control. Make changes as necessary. Even if one person is responsible for paying the bills, make sure that the other one at least knows what is going on and can take over if needed. Consider rotating the bill paying duties every so often.

For your taxes, you may need to make adjustments. Are you currently filing single? Will you file jointly as a married couple or as single but married? Are you increasing or decreasing your deductions? Should you change your exemptions/withholdings now that there are two breadwinners in the house? If you are not sure, the Internal Revenue Service has a withholding calculator at IRS.gov that you can access for free. And I can't say this enough—always consult your tax advisor about these changes.

You also need to decide whose medical insurance you will use—not based on cost, but on coverage. If you have a preexisting condition, make sure it will still be covered if you are changing your insurance carrier. It's good to think about what would happen if one of you lost your job or became disabled. It's not a fun topic, but all the cards should be on the table when it comes to planning your future together. Could either of you survive on just one of your salaries? Does your employer provide for short-term or long-term disability, and what percentage of your salary does it cover?

Chapter 4

The Tax-Deductible Wedding

Most of us never think about tax deductions, even when we are doing our taxes, so the whole idea of tax deductions for your wedding will probably raise a lot of questions. You are probably wondering how this is plausible. Think of it this way: It's the same concept as donating clothes to the Salvation Army or Goodwill or attending a charity dinner. Portions of donations to nonprofit organizations are tax deductible (the organization will tell you how much). So why not take advantage of this benefit in the tax code and kick it up a notch? Donate your dresses or use a location run by a charitable organization. You could save yourself a lot of money. I will repeat this often, but check with your tax advisor about how to get deductions, and never assume anything. To address many of the questions and concerns you might have about this subject, I will review what exactly tax deductions are for charitable organizations.

Tax-Deductible Wedding Q and A

Why don't more people know about the possibility of having a tax-deductible wedding? Most people overlook tax deductions or don't know how to use them to lower the cost of their wedding. They wonder, "Can I get in trouble for writing off wedding expenses?" The answer is no; it is perfectly legal to deduct donations to charitable, tax-exempt 501(c)(3) organizations if the following conditions are met: you get a receipt for the donation from the nonprofit (this receipt must include the name, address, and contact information of the organization; the purpose of the donation; the date, time, and amount of the donation; the signature of someone from the nonprofit; and an itemized list of what specific fees are deductible and which ones are not), and the nonprofit provides you with a statement about how much of the total donation is tax deductible. It would probably also be a good idea to include the BEO (Banquet Event Order), site rental contract, and any other documentation the organization recommends. As always when dealing with tax and legal issues, get the advice of a CPA, attorney, or other tax expert. (Get their opinions or recommendations in writing, too, if you think that makes a difference.)

So what exactly is the definition of a charitable organization? According to the IRS's Exemption Requirement rules posted on IRS.gov: "To be tax-exempt under section 501(c)(3) of the Internal Revenue Code, an organization must be organized and operated exclusively for exempt purposes set forth in section 501(c)(3), and none of its earnings may inure to any private shareholder or individual. Organizations described in section 501(c)(3) are commonly referred to as charitable organizations. Organizations described in section 501(c)(3), other than testing for public safety organizations, are eligible to receive tax-deductible contributions in accordance with Code section 170." The IRS definition continues by stating that "the organization must not be organized or operated for the benefit of private interests, and no part of a section 501(c)(3) organization's net earnings may inure to the benefit of any private shareholder or individual. If the organization engages in an excess benefit transaction with a person having substantial influence over the organization, an excise tax may be imposed on the person and any organization managers agreeing to the transaction."

NOTE: Not all donations to nonprofits can be claimed as charitable deductions, even if they are registered as 501(c)(3) organizations. Check with the organization about what is or isn't tax deductible, because they are required to know this and provide this information to all donors. Don't be afraid to ask; they are used to this, and no one, neither the donor nor the organization, ever wants to bring the wrath of the IRS down on them.

So if all of this tax stuff has you a little nervous about whether or not a nonprofit donation is deductible, you are probably wondering, "How can I verify a nonprofit's status with the IRS?" If you still want to verify further, you can contact the IRS directly by phone at (800) 829-1040. Their hours of operation are Monday through Friday 7:00 a.m. to 10:00 p.m. Officially, there is not a list of what is or is not tax deductible by organization, but according to the IRS, "Charitable contributions are deductible only if you itemize deductions on Form 1040, Schedule A." In addition, there isn't any way to just e-mail someone at the IRS to find out how much or what is deductible at any one organization, but the IRS does state that, "To be deductible, charitable contributions must be made to qualified organizations. See Publication 526, *Charitable Contributions*. If your contribution entitles you to merchandise, goods, or services, including admission to a charity ball, banquet, theatrical performance, or sporting event, you can deduct only the amount that exceeds the fair market value of the benefit received." Their explanation continues by stating, "For a contribution of cash, check, or other monetary gift (regardless of amount) to be deductible, you must maintain as a record of the contribution, have either a bank record or a written communication from the donee organization containing the date and amount of the contribution and the name of the donee." Whatever you do, make sure you keep good records and receipts for any and all monetary donations or other contributions.

The IRS doesn't require receipts for cash donations under $250, but you should keep donation information on file anyway. The IRS states, "for any contribution of $250 or more (including contributions of property), you must obtain a contemporaneous written acknowledgment from the qualified organization. One document may satisfy both the written communication requirement for monetary gifts and the contemporaneous written acknowledgement requirement for all contributions of $250 or more." Either way, it is best to keep all receipts under and over $250, but always check with your attorney and tax advisor to be sure.

You will need to keep complete and accurate records in order to count fees or donations as tax deductions.

What if you forget to get a receipt for something? You will need to keep complete and accurate records in order to count fees or donations as tax deductions. If you lose your receipt, notify the organization immediately and ask them to send you a duplicate. Once you receive it, be sure to make a copy, because you will need to keep the original to file your taxes. That way your tax preparer will have a copy, and so will you if, God forbid, you ever get audited by the IRS.

Where can you find information on IRS deductions online? In addition to doing a search of IRS.gov, you can go to WorldWideWebTax.com, which has directories of exemptions, charitable deductions (which includes the kinds of deductions related to your wedding), and just about anything else related to taxes. The benefit of this site is that it is easier to search and navigate than the IRS Web site.

Now that we have settled that issue, you are most likely asking yourself, "How far in advance should I start planning my tax-deductible wedding?" There is no specific time frame, but you should give yourself some lead time so that you can adequately research which venues will allow you to deduct rental fees, etc. As with any other kind of wedding, the more planning and lead time you have to get organized, the better off you will be. Most people say that a year is sufficient, but only you can decide how much time you will need.

Tax-Deductible Wedding Expenses

Bridal Gowns and Bridesmaids' Dresses

There are many categories of expenses that are tax deductible, but when it comes to weddings, the single most popular, stressed over, and emotional purchase is the wedding gown, so that is where we will start. One of the most popular ways to get a tax deduction is to donate your wedding gown or all of those bridesmaids' dresses that are collecting dust (and perhaps a little bit of resentment, right?). You'll feel good knowing that the proceeds will go toward various charities and notable causes, and the dresses (as well as any shipping costs to send the dresses to the charities) are tax deductible. Some of the best sites for donating dresses include BridalGarden.com, where the proceeds from the sale of your donated dress benefit disadvantaged children via the Sheltering Arms Children's Service, and BridesAgainstBreastCancer.org, which sells preowned bridal gowns at trunk shows all over the country and uses the proceeds to grant wishes for terminally ill breast cancer patients. MakingMemories.org and IDoFoundation.org also accept donated wedding dresses and sell them to help fund the work of charities on their list of recipients.

If your bridesmaids want to help a good cause, they can donate their dresses to CinderellaProject.net, which donates the dresses to girls who can't afford to buy prom dresses. Another way to help others is to donate not just bridesmaids' dresses, but purses, shoes, and other accessories. PrincessProject.org has a listing of charities around the country that take donations, including accessories, so that underprivileged girls can have a chance to wear nice things at their prom.

For the ultimate in recycling, you may also be able to find wedding items at your local Salvation Army or Goodwill if you want to go vintage or don't want to buy a new gown. I know of one woman who was able to buy her barely used bridal gown, headpiece, and a rehearsal dinner dress from a secondhand store. Think about it—you will save money and give to a good cause, and when you are finished, you can donate the dress again and begin the process all over for another bride. Depending on whether or not you itemize and the resale store items are deductible, you could get a deduction for buying and donating. What goes around comes around, right?

Location, Location, Location

Brides and grooms spend hours looking at brochures, visiting venues, and fantasizing about where their ceremony and reception will be held. Did you know that your wedding reception site can be tax deductible? Most couples have no idea. There are many options to choose from when picking out a ceremony and/or reception venue, and if you decide to go with something less traditional, you could save some money. How, you ask? Read on, and be sure to speak to your accountant and see what venues count as a tax deduction.

Having your wedding at an alternative venue can be an elegant, original way to set your wedding apart and make a statement about your personal tastes. Some offbeat or less mainstream wedding venues that are tax deductible can be fascinating and charming places for weddings, and because they are often unique or distinct architecturally, they may require less fuss over decorations. Using a 501(c)(3) charitable organization for your reception could mean a tax write-off on the facility fee, which for tax purposes the IRS considers a donation to the organization. As always, remember to con-

married at the Aquarium
with attendant fishes

sult the organization before you move too far along, and always ask your tax advisor any additional questions you may have.

Some fun and interesting alternatives for your wedding venue include museums, national parks, botanical gardens, wildlife preserves, historic sites, aquariums, and zoos. Since these places obviously don't specialize in weddings, you'll want to ask the following questions before you make your choice:

- Is there a limit to the number of guests that can be invited?

- How far in advance must the wedding reservation be booked? Is there a waiting list?

- Are there special rates for reserving a place extra early?

- Are pets allowed? (Some brides and grooms like to include their pet in the wedding ceremony.)

- Are there any restrictions for getting married there on a weekend or on a major holiday?

- Are there restrictions on the length of time of the wedding?

- Is alcohol permitted on the premises?

- Who will be responsible for cleanup?

- Are permits necessary? If so, what kinds of permits are required, what is the deadline for obtaining them, and how much do they cost?

- Does the site have preferred caterers or entertainment?

- What equipment/services/rental will be part of the wedding package?

- Will there be designated parking for guests?

- Is nearby lodging available for long-distance travelers?

- What part of the package will be considered tax deductible?

Whether you hold the ceremony in a place of worship or a more nontraditional location, try to find a reception venue that is a 501(c)(3) charitable organization, because you may be able to deduct the costs. The reception is one of the single largest costs of a wedding, in some cases as much as 50 percent of the total cost. When you consider that the average wedding costs around $26,000, that is nothing to sneeze at.

Before you book the site for your wedding, insist on seeing the organization's letter of exemption from the IRS, the notice of official status as a charitable organization. (Again, don't be shy about this; it is just part of the process of being a nonprofit and having your status verified by donors. People who work for nonprofits are used to being asked pointed questions about taxes, their standing, and so on, and they are obligated to provide this information anyway.) In addition, make sure that you get details about your fees, what amount of the facility fees are deductible (this information always comes from the nonprofit), the amount you paid, and an acknowledgement letter that says you made a donation. Every site is different and has different amounts that are deductible, so it's a good idea to find out this kind of information up front as you are searching for venues. You don't want to set your sights on a place to find out later that the deduction won't offset the fee. Also, before you make a deposit or pay any money, get a contract or letter of agreement that clearly defines the fees, rules, and other important details.

The reception is one of the single largest costs of a wedding, in some cases as much as 50 percent of the total cost.

Museums

Museums are a lovely wedding venue, and their diverse architecture provide a varied selection of design aesthetics to match the style of your wedding. I love them because they are repositories of such interesting things; it's always a joy to be in the presence of valuable artifacts, priceless art, and cultural treasures. To me, the top three museums I would love to have as a wedding venue are the Metropolitan Museum of Art in New York City, the Getty in Los Angeles, and Chrysler Hall in Norfolk, Virginia.

If you think a wedding in a museum might be an intriguing option to consider, don't hesitate to find out more. It's very simple to do if you familiarize yourself with your local museums first. Then, if you are sure this is what you want to do, you can find more museums to review by going to the American Association of Museums's national directory at www.aam-us.org. Again, the use of the facility will be a tax deduction if the museum is a charitable organization and the rental of the facility is considered a donation.

Museums are such popular places for events that they have become very sophisticated at handling the arrangements and helping plan the event, and many have full-time event staff. There can be some restrictions about the use of the space, however, because of the value and rarity of the museum's contents. You don't want Uncle Joe accidentally knocking over a Grecian sculpture from the fifth century B.C., now do you?

When it comes to museum rentals, the following are some questions you should ask:

- How much of the donation is tax deductible?

- Are outside caterers allowed, or is there a list of approved caterers that must be used?

- Are alcoholic beverages allowed? If so, can red wine be served? (Fears over stains abound.)

- Is liability insurance required?

- What happens if any of the artwork is damaged during the event?

Work closely with the museum representative throughout your planning, and you shouldn't have any problems. The staff will be there to keep you abreast on all of the rules and restrictions.

National Parks

National parks are a wonderful venue for weddings—there really isn't much you can improve on when it comes to a bucolic natural setting. Who needs decorations when you have Mother Nature's handiwork? The National Park

Service's Web site, www.nps.gov, includes a huge directory of local, state, and national parks that you can choose from to host your wedding. Simply type "weddings" into the search box, and you will find tons of information and links about holding weddings in a national park. Be sure to find out if the park has special package deals for weddings, which can often be a great way to save money. Also make sure to call the park directly to find out about the current location, space use policies, requirements, and restrictions.

Most importantly, make sure you ask about use permits. While each national park property is different, most have some sort of permit requirement, which is designed to protect the park's natural beauty and cultural resources. The park staff want to make the park available to the public and are reluctant to deny visitors access, but at the same time they don't want precious resources damaged, and they are mandated to preserve the park's tranquility. Other permits that may be required could relate to managing crowd densities, discouraging the consumption of alcoholic beverages, and preventing any conflicts with existing programs offered on-site. You can also find out more about having a wedding in national parks or wilderness areas by going to GORP.away.com, which is devoted to outdoor and nature travel. It has one of the most extensive online listings of national parks, forests, monuments, nature preserves, wildlife refuges, trails, rivers, lakes, and historic sites.

Botanical Gardens, Public Gardens, and Arboreta

Botanical gardens, public gardens, and arboreta are also popular options for wedding venues. Just as with museums, botanical gardens and arboreta often have extensive public spaces and most likely charge some kind of facility fee. Luckily for us, this fee is tax deductible, and the grounds fees (for surrounding lawn and grounds) may also be tax deductible. If you would like to research these kinds of venues, the National Association of Botanical Gardens and Arboretums' Web site, www.publicgardens.org, has a listing of botanical gardens and arboreta nationwide that is searchable by state. You could also do a keyword search for "weddings" and see if anything comes up. Some places allow weddings, but not all do, so if you can't tell whether or not weddings are allowed at a particular garden, pick up the phone and give them a call. For example, the U.S. Botanic Garden in Washington, D.C., clearly states that they don't allow weddings (surprising, isn't it?), but Meadowlark Botanical Gardens in Vienna, Virginia—which is not far from D.C.—does. This popular wedding destination has a yearlong waiting list, but the wait is often worth it because the dedicated event staff does a great job and the setting is incredible. (The rental fee may be tax deductible, too.)

Zoos

Zoos, unique and exotic, are not unheard of as a venue for wedding receptions. They are wonderful places where wedding guests can have some fun and commune with nature in a beautiful setting. In my area, the Maryland Zoo, in Baltimore, Maryland, features the Mansion House Porch, a private glass-enclosed veranda and solarium that is closed to the public during events so you don't have to worry about visitors wandering through your reception. It has been the scene of many happy weddings, and Baltimore's own Duff Goldman (of *Ace of Cakes* fame) has made many cakes for the zoo. (If you would like to find out more about this zoo, you can go to their Web site, www.marylandzoo.org. If you want to find other zoos that host weddings, you can search the directory on the Association of Zoos and Aquariums' Web site, www.aza.org.)

This is just one example of what's out there, and each zoo has its own policies, fees, and ways of hosting weddings, so do your research. It pays to know what the going rates are in your area for more mainstream locations, so that way you can compare the true cost and determine if a nontraditional venue is the way you really want to go. You also need to verify the nonprofit status with the meeting or event planner. As with any rental space, there will be fees, rules, and restrictions, so be sure to ask questions. The following are some questions you can ask of the zoo's event-planning staff:

It pays to know what the going rates are in your area for more mainstream locations, so that way you can compare the true cost and determine if a nontraditional venue is the way you really want to go.

- Is it okay to bring in outside caterers?

- What times and days are weddings held? Is it only after the zoo is closed?

- Can guests receive a tour of the zoo before the wedding?

- Is there special parking for wedding guests?

- Are pets allowed? (Some brides and grooms like their pets to participate in their wedding.)

Historic Sites

Hosting a wedding at a historic location can not only help educate your guests, but it will give them something to do while you and the rest of the wedding party are busy having your photographs taken. The directory of historic house museums at MuseumsUSA.org lists hundreds of historic houses in each state, and some of these venues are so popular for events that they have their own staff of special-events planners. You can click on the Web site of the location for information about event planning or contact the venue directly. As with other nonprofit venues, the facility fee may be tax deductible as a donation for the upkeep of the historic property. Always ask a lot of questions up front about cost, hours of operation, and whether or not the venue is open to the public during your reception, and get everything in writing.

Aquariums and Wildlife Preserves

For those who like to take a walk on the wild side, hosting a reception at an aquarium or wildlife preserve may be an intriguing alternative. In many cases, the facility or rental fees for ceremony and reception spaces go toward maintaining the animals' natural habitat, care, and, in some cases, preservation of endangered species and other programs. To find an aquarium in your area, go to the Association of Zoos and Aquariums Web site, www.aza.org, and search their directory by location. Once you find an aquarium in your area, look up their Web site and see if they do weddings. If they do, then give them a call and see if you can ask some questions on the phone.

If things seem promising, go and see the venue, meet the event-planning staff, and find out what you need to know. As always, remember to consult the organization to find out if any of the fees are tax deductible before you move too far along, and always ask your tax advisor about any additional questions you may have.

Ministry Services

When it comes time to pay the officiant for conducting your wedding ceremony, the cost of this may be tax deductible if the check is made payable directly to the house of worship. The reason for this is that the fee is considered an honorarium that is earmarked for services and contributions that are tax deductible. If the check is made out to the clergy directly, then that is *not* tax deductible, because he or she is not a tax-exempt charitable organization. In other words, the check made out to St. John's Episcopal Church can be deducted, but a check made out to Pastor Bob is not tax deductible. As with all things related to the IRS, check with a tax expert, CPA, or attorney to make sure if something is tax deductible.

Gift Giving That Gives Back

Who doesn't love a fabulous party? It's even more fun when the party is in your honor and you are the one receiving all of the gifts! But before the shower and wedding gifts start pouring in, think about asking your guests to make a donation in your name to a charity of your choice instead. Of course, this is supposed to be your special day, and everyone loves receiving presents, so don't feel bad if you don't want to participate in this tax-deductible option. Now, if this is not your first marriage, you've probably already received a wedding whatchamacallit or two as gifts, or you got a gift, but it wasn't really your taste. In this case regifting is in good taste because it goes to a worthy cause. There are only so many gifts a person can really want or need anyway, right? If you do this, then you'll feel good about helping out someone in need.

You can also choose to make a charitable donation in honor of your guests in lieu of buying wedding favors, and/or set up a charitable gift registry. (These are two of the biggest wedding trends in recent years.) For

example, if you make a donation to the American Diabetes Association (which is tax deductible, by the way) instead of purchasing wedding favors, they will send you complimentary invitation or tent cards. Imagine how thoughtful it would be if you took the same amount of money you would have spent on favors, say $2.00 to $5.00 dollars per guest, and donated that amount in your guests' names. That is certainly more memorable than a trifle that your guests will either lose or forget the next day.

In terms of gift registries, the I Do Foundation has a great gift registry program where they link with major consumer product partners to offer brides and grooms the chance to make a difference when they shop. If they register with one of the I Do Foundation's corporate partner stores, such as Mikasa, Cooking.com, Target, REI, Bloomingdale's, Macy's, and others, then from 2 to 10 percent of your guests' purchases will be donated to a charity of your choice. Go to www.idofoundation.org to learn more about this great program and select a charity from one of their lists.

JustGive.org is another site that allows couples to create a unique and meaningful gift registry, used alone or in addition to traditional gift registries. Couples can create a customized Web site that encourages contributions to their favorite charities, and JustGive.org offers more than one million charities for couples to choose from, including national and local organizations.

Yet another way to give back is to have your registry at one of the fair trade Web sites, like TenThousandVillages.org. Everything for sale on their site is fair trade and protects the work of local artisans, preserves ancient artistic traditions and techniques, and ensures that a significant portion of the sale of goods goes directly back to the artisans so that they can earn a livable wage and not be exploited by outside interests. While this may not be tax deductible, your guests' money goes to a good cause and in your name.

Wedding Leftovers—Do Not Let It Go to Waste!

Now that the big day is over, what to do with all the leftovers? Food, flowers, and unwanted wedding accessories can all be donated.

Food

Leftover appetizers, entrees, bread, condiments, fruit, cheese, desserts, etc. from your wedding can be donated to a local shelter or food bank/food pantry, which can be found at FoodPantries.org. For example, America's Second Harvest has a network of over two hundred food banks that they distribute food to on a daily basis. Before you decide you want to donate leftovers to a food bank, clear it with the caterer, because they will have to prepare the food for pickup, and each group has different requirements about what kinds of food can be donated, in what form, and in what kind of containers. Call the food bank for any rules and restrictions. The following are some questions to ask before you offer to donate anything:

- How will they get the food? Will they pick it up, or will you have to deliver it?

- What food (hot/cold, perishable/nonperishable) items can be donated?

- Is this donation tax deductible? Are they a 501(c)(3)?

- What times and days of the week do they accept food?

- Does the food need to be packaged in a particular way or in certain kinds of containers?

- What kinds of food won't they accept?

It is highly likely this donation is tax deductible, but check with the food bank and your tax preparer first.

Flowers

Rather than just toss the flowers out after your wedding, why not donate them to a hospice or other charitable hospital? Chances are the cost of the flowers, if donated to a charitable organization, will be deductible.

Accessories

You'll likely want to keep certain items from your special day to remember it by—perhaps your "something blue" or a cherished family heirloom you wore—but there will definitely be other items that you'll never use again. If they are not particularly sentimental, such as your wedding shoes, the handbag you used for the dollar dance (if you had one), or even that slip that kept shifting around when you walked, you can find a consignment shop that donates proceeds to charities such as Goodwill or the Salvation

Army. Not only will you help out a good cause, but another bride-to-be will be ecstatic to find a bargain or two. Also, if you have any leftover balloons or balloon sculptures that you used to decorate the reception site with, you may want to consider donating them to a local children's hospital or to a Ronald McDonald House. You could brighten someone's day.

Honeymoons

Well, we are not finished yet. You probably thought we were at the end of the tax-deduction possibilities, but I have saved the best for last: Your honeymoon can also yield a tax deduction. What better way to get closer to your main squeeze than by taking off on a honeymoon and the adventure of a lifetime, all for a good cause? Read on.

Going Global for a Tax Deduction

Global Volunteers is a private, nonprofit, nonsectarian development organization founded in 1984 with the goal of helping to establish a foundation for peace through mutual international understanding. They offer a short-term service program that places volunteers in twenty countries worldwide.

Volunteers can give of their time for one to six weeks, living with local people and having a truly life-affirming experience. The volunteer work experience can take place in Asia, Africa, Latin America, the Caribbean, Europe, or the United States. They can work on all sorts of projects that range from building classrooms in Ghana to teaching business courses in the Ukraine or teaching English in China. No experience is necessary (except for those working in medical programs).

To participate, volunteers pay a U.S. tax-deductible fee that covers food, lodging, transportation at the site, the services of an experienced team leader, and project materials. Transportation to and from sites is not included, although airfare is tax deductible. You can expect to work on average about eight hours a day, five days a week (evening and weekends are free for volunteers to explore and get to know their host country), and you should keep track of the number of hours you worked and out of pocket expenses, which are tax deductible. Your out-of-pocket savings for travel can be substantial as a volunteer, because your service program fees, airfare, visa, and related travel expenses are generally tax deductible for U.S. taxpayers. The principal reason you receive this benefit as a U.S. taxpayer is that you are donating your time to a nonprofit, and if they had to pay you or someone else, it would be a large sum of money.

Build a Home for Someone Else Before You Start Living in Yours
Doing something together that reinforces your shared values helps to deepen your bond, and this can be a great activity to do during your honeymoon. One way to do that is to help someone else realize his or her dream of owning a home. Habitat for Humanity International (www.habitat.org) has helped build homes for thousands of people who, due to financial hardship, might not ever have owned their own home.

Planning and organizing, figuring out how to do a budget, estimating how much your wedding will cost, determining what is tax deductible—I think we have covered all of the parts of the initial phase of planning your wedding. The next important area to cover is how to save *for* your wedding and how to save *on* your wedding. Because if you don't have a plan for this part, you will not be able to get to your final destination—the altar.

Chapter 5

Savings You Never Knew Existed

How do you start saving for wedding expenses? That's a good question! This chapter is about saving (in other words, setting money aside) for your wedding and finding ways to trim costs. As we discussed in chapters 3 and 4, it is important to try to save as much discretionary income (income you have left after you pay bills) as you can before the planning for the festivities begins. Select checking accounts, savings accounts, investments, and other vehicles that will earn you interest. Certificates of deposit (CDs) and money market funds are other options, but be sure to shop for the best rates. Do the research at your own bank and compare your bank's interest-earning products with those of other banks. BankRate.com has many articles about how to shop around for the best rates on money market accounts and how to find one that fits your budget, goals, and lifestyle.

How to Save for Your Wedding

You need to have a strategy for saving money and finding additional money that you can use to pay for your wedding. A joint savings account will provide you with interest, but rates are rarely higher than 2 percent. Let's look at a few other financial products that may work.

Certificates of Deposit (CDs)

CDs have different maturity levels ranging from three months to three years. (There even may be some that are longer than three years; it just depends on what is offered.) Check around at various banks to see what their maturity rates are. Think about your wedding date, the expenses you'll incur, and how long you'd like to keep the CD active. Another bonus with starting up a CD is if there is any money left over after your wedding, you can use it toward the down payment on a dream home or save it for another big purchase.

Treasury Securities

When I hear the words *savings bond,* I think of being a kid and getting a savings bond for my birthday. Are they still around? Yes. In fact, treasury securities, which include bonds, are a safe investment. They are backed by the government, and although they yield lower rates than other kinds of investments, they aren't a bad idea if you are saving for your wedding. Depending on how and where you purchase them, the fee to maintain them while they mature may be tax deductible—but the securities and bonds themselves are not. If you go to TreasuryDirect.gov, you can purchase bonds direct from the government, and they will help you maintain the bonds until they mature.

The following is a list of common treasury securities and the minimum purchase amount:

Treasury bills	$100
Treasury notes	$100
EE/E savings bonds	$25
I savings bonds	$25 if purchased via TreasuryDirect.gov; $50 if purchased as paper bond certificate
HH/H savings bonds	n/a

Source: TreasuryDirect.gov

Friends and Family

Another wedding trend is having others—other than just the couples' parents—help foot the bill for the wedding. More people are looking to their friends and other relatives to help pitch in, and banks and other companies have designed registries with this in mind. For example, the DreamBuilder savings account from Mercantile Bank (www.mercantilebk.com/personal/bc/dreambuilder-choice.php) works like a normal wedding registry, but people can donate money to your account. You simply open the account for $50, and your relatives and friends can donate money directly to your account to help with the wedding. These payments can be made online, by mail, or in person.

IRAs and 401(k)s: As They Say on *The Sopranos,* Fuggedaboudit

Thinking about using your Individual Retirement Account (IRA) and/or 401(k) to pay for your wedding? Well, don't. This is the last thing that you should ever do. Not only will you incur severe penalties if you take money out before you are supposed to, but once you dip into your IRA or 401(k), it can be very hard to put your finances back together again. This is your nest egg for the future, and we all know what happened to Humpty Dumpty. This book provides so many other ways to finance your wedding that you shouldn't even need to consider this.

Easy Ways to Save for Your Wedding

When it comes to finding simple, quick, or easy ways to save money on a daily basis, you might not be able to think of things that seem to make a big enough contribution to your wedding budget. If you are serious about saving and you use the worksheets that have already been mentioned, you will be able to cut your costs every day and probably won't even notice or feel the pinch. Here is one way to quickly see how even small things can add up: Say you go to a fancy coffee shop every morning for your half-caf, no foam, whatever. If the cost of that one cup of coffee is $3.58 including tax, that comes to $930.80 in a year. Not bad for just cutting out a cup of store-bought coffee. Here are some other suggestions:

- Limit eating out; bring your lunch to work.

- Cut out or lessen your trips to fancy coffee shops, drink cheaper coffee, or make your own coffee. (This will save money on gas, too.)

- Clip coupons. It's like free money, and over time it can really save a lot in your budget.

- Sell unwanted clothing and other items through a consignment store. They will sell your wares, and you get a percentage of the profits. (As with anything, always make sure that you get the store's terms and agreements in writing and that you understand how you will be paid and how often.)

- Sell unwanted items on eBay.com or Craigslist.org.

- Think about what marketable skills or talents you might have that you can turn into freelancing opportunities. There are lots of sites, such as Elance.com, Craigslist.org, and Guru.com, that let you post your services for free.

- Try bartering for things that you would normally buy. This can save money on your regular expenses, and the savings can be put toward your wedding. Join bartering clubs to save on a host of products and services.

- Ask your parents if you can clean out their garage or attic and have a yard sale with their treasures. I'm sure you also have some items stored at your parents' house that they would love to see go. Ask them if a percentage of your sales can go towards your wedding. Who knows—you may get lucky, and they will donate their percentage to your wedding.

How to Trim Costs

Now that you know a little bit about how to save *for* your wedding, we need to talk about how to save *on* the wedding. Every penny you can save now will help you pay later for other things that you consider a priority. There are a lot of Web sites out there that have ideas for how to bring down the costs of your wedding, but some of the better ones include FrugalBride.com and WedFrugal.com.

One of the first things that you can do to get the costs of the wedding down is to reduce the number of guests. This single act, aside from getting the reception venue for free, will bring the costs down significantly.

One of the first things that you can do to get the costs of the wedding down is to reduce the number of guests.

Having the wedding during off-season or on off days like Friday, a weeknight, or Sunday, can result in huge savings because vendors will give you a better deal when things are slow. Off times can also reduce the cost of hiring caterers, renting a venue, and rental equipment.

Rather than pay for all of the services you need, such as musicians, the officiant, or DJ, see who you and your support team might know that could do some of these things for free as part of their role in the day's festivities. For example, if you have a cousin who plays in a band, see if she will ask some of her fellow musicians to play at your reception. Nowadays, almost anyone can be ordained as a minister online, and this might be a task a friend would like to do.

Where possible, rent rather than buy things like jewelry, accessories, clothing, and equipment. Some Web sites that do this include AdornBrides .com and Avelle (www.bagborroworsteal.com).

Don't forget to think beyond the traditional bridal store and check out stores like Target, JCPenney, and J Crew, all of which have wedding attire and styles that can be worn by the bridal party, as well as wholesale stores such as Costco, Sam's Club, and Wal-Mart. I encourage you to have an open mind and give these stores a try if you're not having much luck elsewhere. You'll save much more money than if you splurged on a once-in-a-lifetime designer gown. You can also go to sites like BravoBride.com and buy new or gently used bridal gowns and accessories.

Of all the expenses for a wedding, nothing comes close to the cost of the reception, and you should try to save money on this part of your budget every chance you get. One way is to save on some of the rental equipment. Ask the venue if they could put you in contact with the couple using the space the same day as you are, either before or after your wedding, so you can discuss possibly sharing the cost of tents, chairs, tables, and rental equipment and decorations.

Flowers can make your budget wilt in no time if you are not careful, so consider doing your own flower arrangements, buying the flowers in season (to find out what flowers are in bloom during what season, ElegantGala .com has a nice list that you can use as a reference), and/or buying from a wholesaler (if they are open to the public). A flower-arrangement class can

teach you how to make arrangements yourself, and this is not just for crafty-types; it's also a fun form of creativity. To make the job easier, have your friends and family help and make a party of it. Order pizza, and use this as a time to create some memories that you can fondly look back on later.

Another way to cut down on the cost of flowers is to use silk flowers entirely or mix them with real flowers to get a more natural look. Many craft retailers, such as Michael's and the Arts & Crafts Store, have wonderful supplies and often provide tips, ideas, and free classes on flower arranging. If you would like to try flower crafts on your own minus the craft store, here is a quick guide on how to make a bouquet on a budget:

1. Practice with supermarket flowers or flowers from a wholesaler to save money.

2. Buy florist's tape, organza, satin ribbon, scissors, and flower pins.

3. Make sure the flowers are placed in water until they are needed.

4. Cut a yard or less of the florist's tape, organza, and satin ribbon, and set them aside.

5. Take your flowers out of the water and dry them.

6. Trim the flowers to your liking.

7. Wrap the flower and greenery stems with florist's tape, followed by organza, and then satin ribbon. Secure the ribbon using the decorative flower pins.

You can also shop at the wholesale florist for other kinds of wedding decoration supplies, such as candles, ribbon, etc. It is also worthwhile to see if any of the wholesale florists in your area offer direct sales to the public online. Search the yellow pages to find a floral wholesaler in your area and give them a call; they may just be willing to work with you.

Invitations can be another huge expense once you add in the postage, printing, and paper, but there are ways to get around this if you are clever. Stay away from engraved or embossed (raised print) invitations and stick to offset (flat) printing on inexpensive paper. There are also a slew of chic, high-quality paper suppliers online that have their own unique style and vibe. Many paper stores, like Paper Divas, now sell high-quality paper and the DIYer can get lots of ideas, supplies, and instructions from Martha Stewart. There are many projects that can be easily printed from your computer that will be fine for less-formal weddings, and if you really want to save money, go with Evite.com, MyPunchBowl.com, or www.pingg.com and send the invitations by e-mail. These programs come with all sorts of templates and let you track your RSVPs; they also make gift suggestions and keep invitees in touch. Best of all, they are free!

In addition to these tips, there are a few specific areas where you can save money on your wedding: the alcohol, the cake, and the honeymoon.

Is It Time for "Cheers!" or What?

What's the second thing that comes to mind when you hear the word *wedding*? No, not love, the bride, or the expense (although those are definitely up there). It's probably alcohol—and lots of it. There will be times when you'll run into fees that aren't exactly tax deductible, and this is probably going to be one of those times. Don't worry; I have you covered. You can buy me a drink at the bar later.

While alcoholic beverages are not tax deductible, there is no reason why you can't save on this expense and be creative at the same time. Shop around for the best deals ahead of time. Wholesalers like BJs, Costco, and Sam's Club often offer decent discounts, and retailers almost always give you case discounts and let you return unopened bottles for a refund.

In addition to open bars and beer and wine service, the latest wedding trend to hit the scene is cocktails. Many couples are opting to create their own signature cocktails instead of having an open bar free-for-all. This limits your drink selection and will save you money. If you're searching for a great drink, see if one of the mixologists at a top-notch local bar will create one for you and put it on their menu to promote your wedding. The drink should reflect something about you and the groom, include ingredients that you like or that have some significance in your life together, and have a name that means something to both of you (like a favorite pet's name, the name of the city where you first met, etc.). To make sure the drinks served at your wedding meet the highest standards, you'll probably need to invest in a few good quality-control experts, such as yourself and your bridesmaids (wink, wink). To learn more about great cocktail recipes, stories, and origins, check out Cocktail.com, DrinkNation.com, and WebTender.com.

The following are types of drinks you could serve that, unlike an open bar, won't break the bank:

- Cocktails and martinis

- Champagne drinks

- Nonalcoholic beverages

- Specialty cocktails

- Rum-tasting bar

- Tequila samplers

- Bellinis

- Elegant punches

Cake Rental

Have you ever thought about renting your wedding cake? Maybe not, or maybe you have never heard of cake rentals. But this is a new trend, and some bakers are offering this service. Here is how it works. You select the

wedding cake you want from several design patterns, which is what will be displayed at the reception. What the guests won't know is that this is a prop with just a top and/or bottom layer for cutting and for the first year anniversary. The cake that will be served is a sheet cake kept in the back, which is definitely much cheaper to make and decorate than a tiered wedding cake. Once the bride and groom do the traditional cake cutting and take photos, the cake is quickly whisked away to the kitchen, out of sight, where the sheet cake will be sliced and plated. The guests are none the wiser, and you will have saved some bucks on your wedding cake.

Another way to save on the cake is to look for alternatives rather than go to an expensive pastry chef. Stores such as Sam's Club, Costco's, and your local supermarket can make cakes to order for a fraction of the cost, and you may be able to negotiate about delivery (but check with the individual store for their policy).

You might also consider the services of a home baker. There are many people who are pretty good bakers, and you should count yourself lucky if you have a Bree Van de Kamp in your neighborhood, like on *Desperate Housewives*. I have a relative who is an awesome baker, and I would certainly pick her moist, delicious cake before any others. If you know of someone in your area who is also a first-rate baker like my relative, then by all means seek her out. Or ask friends, your church group, or your book club if they know of someone. Why pay higher prices for your wedding cake if you do not have to?

Have a Traditional Honeymoon for Less

If you want a traditional honeymoon, there are ways to save on this part of the wedding, too.

Honeymoon Registries

Why not have someone else pay for it? Well, sort of. Web sites such as HoneyLuna.com, Traveler's Joy (www.travelersjoy.com), TheBigDay.com, and others allow couples to set up registries where wedding guests can chip in for the honeymoon. It works just like your gift registry. You set up the parts of your honeymoon that need to be paid for, and your guests can contribute as much or as little as they like. The registry can cover travel costs, like airline tickets, or leisure activities like whale watching, scuba diving, or a candlelit dinner for two.

Home Exchange/Swapping

If, in addition to your honeymoon registry, you want to get other parts of the honeymoon covered on your own, like your lodging, why not trade your house for someone else's in a destination that you have always wanted to visit? You could potentially swap houses with someone in Tuscany while they are visiting your hometown and staying at your home. You can do this by going through a service such as HomeExchange.com, a house-swapping service that, while not new, has only recently become more mainstream. HomeExchange.com costs $99 a year, but it lists properties around the world. You should also check out International Home Exchange (www.ihen.com). It also has a membership fee, but it's much lower ($39 a year), and essentially it works pretty much the same way as HomeExchange.com does.

House-Sitting

House-sitting for someone is another lodging option that you could consider. I have only house-sat for relatives or watched over my neighbor's house, but I do know that this is a popular way to get free lodging. If you have a relative in a really desirable location, like Hawaii, ask them if you can house-sit for them while they are on vacation—but do it long before you begin making your wedding plans, because you both will need plenty of lead time to plan and coordinate times, dates, flights, and so on. Also ask other family members and friends if they know of someone who needs a house sitter. Lastly, you could try a service to help you find a house to sit for, such as HouseCares.com, which can connect you with folks in need of a house sitter almost anywhere around the world.

Hostels

Overall, I think you will find that today's hostels are not like the ones your parents knew and dreaded. Now they are clean, modern, and equipped with all of the modern conveniences. While there have been horror movies made about hostel guests whose experiences left them scarred for life, hostels really are great places to stay and are very economical. Nowadays they aren't just made for broke, unbathed students, and many hostels cater to adults, families, and older adults. You can often book online and view what the hostel and rooms look like where you will be staying. There are often reviews posted by actual visitors to the hostel, which can be an invaluable source of useful information. Hostelworld.com has a yearly hostel ranking, but ultimately only you can decide if you want to take the high- or low-rent road.

If you're considering a hostel, here are some questions to ask before you make a reservation:

- What types of rooms (e.g., dormitory, private, single, double) are available?

- What types of beds (e.g., bunk, twin, queen) are available?

- Do you have to bring your own towels and bed linens?

- Is there a curfew and if so what time?

- Are there lockers for guests' use?

- Is there a wireless or Internet connection?

- Are there private or communal bathrooms? If the latter, how many people to a bathroom?

Cruise Lecturer and Instructor

Have you ever wondered how you could get a free trip on a cruise ship? As far-fetched as it may sound, it is a very real possibility. An easy way to do it is as a lecturer, golf teacher, wine educator, or yoga teacher. Whatever kind of topic, hobby, or interest you can think of that you might have a special skill in, this might be your opportunity to turn it into a free cruise. On the face of it this may seem simple, but you need to be prepared and present yourself with confidence and professionalism. It is worth it, though, if you get selected, because you and your spouse can travel for free on your honeymoon with little effort and can continue to do so year after year.

Most trips are free to instructors, but some have an administrative fee of $65 to $100 a day. But if you are able to bring along a guest free of charge, it is well worth the money. According to SixthStar.com, a marketing entertainment firm out of Fort Lauderdale, Florida, that books cruise entertainment, the average lecturer must provide three to four lectures that are thirty-five minutes in length with about ten minutes of Q and A. Audience sizes range from fifty to three hundred people and the guest lecturers can have a range of skills and talents, from knowledge of the Great Barrier Reef to Texas Hold 'Em. What matters is that the audience is interested in the subject matter and that the guest speaker is knowledgeable, engaging, and begins and ends on time. Cruise ships are always looking for someone who can capture the audience's attention, and it doesn't matter whether the presenter is a face painter, photographer, or comedian. Before you apply, ask the booker what kinds of qualifications they are looking for. Who knows— you just might be setting sail soon.

Freight and Cargo Travel

Freight travel is like running away with the circus on a boat. You can travel for six months or more without making a lot of stops, and the cost is quite affordable. Although freight and cargo ships do carry passengers, their real purpose is to deliver goods and services to different countries. If you decide to go this route, expect that the average price per person is about $70 to $100 a day, which is a pretty good deal. Depending on the ship, some meals may be included with your stay, but this is something you should negotiate and firm up before you ever hand over any money or leave port. As with anything else, make sure you get everything in writing before you sign the dotted line.

Because they aren't passenger ships, these boats can usually only carry a small group of people, say up to twelve passengers at most. When you arrive on board, be prepared to find accommodations that don't even come close to those found on a cruise ship. Your stateroom will be small and very basic, but it should be clean, and sheets, furniture, and other items in the room should be in good condition. It's not likely that you will find any entertainment on board, but the two of you should be able to come up with your own entertainment (you are on your honeymoon, right?). What is also different from a cruise ship is the less orchestrated feel of life on board; the travel will be much more laid-back and easygoing. Just think of it as if you were backpacking through Europe, but on a freight ship. If you plan to do some lengthy travel on land once you arrive, some ships have the added benefit of letting you bring your car or motorbike on board (for a fee, of course). I like the fact that this type of travel experience lets you relax and see the world on your own terms, which always makes for more interesting travel. Some cargo and freight companies to check out are Maris Freighter & Specialty Cruises (www.freightercruises.com), Freighter World Cruises (www.freighterworld.com), and TravLtips (www.travltips.com).

Courier Travel

Years ago, only a few people in the know had any idea how to travel as a courier, a very specific form of travel primarily meant to get a package or product from point A to point B via air travel on commercial airlines. It may not be glamorous, but you can save money on airfare to an expensive destination like Hawaii. The money you save can be spent on fun things like helicopter rides over the island, snorkeling, or staying at a chichi resort. Think of yourself as the UPS guy: You help the courier company out by delivering their important documents and packages safely, and in return you get a discounted flight.

On the face of it, this method of package delivery may seem exorbitant, but for some companies the cost is not as important as the security of knowing that their package was delivered to its final destination by a real person. Sometimes the products being couriered are so valuable, time sensitive, or essential to the operations of the company that peace of mind is worth the cost of paying someone to hand deliver the package. Here is how it works. You reserve your flight on a regular airline that has agreements with courier companies for reduced ticket prices for their couriers. (The ticket price discount can range from 50 to 85 percent off the normal price.) Once your flight has been confirmed, you make your payment to the courier. You receive your ticket on the day of the flight—either at the airport from a representative of the courier company or at the courier company's offices. Once you reach your destination, you hand over the shipping document to a shipping agent and go about your merry way.

While all of this may seem like covert operations, the exchange of the package in question is between legitimate, established companies that have used people to convey packages this way for years. You are just discreetly delivering a package—you don't get to peek at what's in it. Most packages are couriered from major cities such as New York, Los Angeles, and Miami, so if you are not near any of those cities or at least a large airport, chances are you will be responsible for your travel arrangements to one of the large metro-area airports.

There are several companies that can match you with a courier company, and some have small yearly membership fees. Some of the better known, more respected booking companies include the International Association of Air Travel Couriers (www.courier.org), A1Express.com, and JupiterAir.com.

If you plan to be a courier and want to travel as a couple, you should coordinate the flight plans with the courier service to see what (or if) you can do to arrive around the same time, or at least the same day. If you can't travel together, you may be able to arrange different travel times and still arrive at the same location, but be prepared for each assignment to have different restrictions. You can get some good deals on international travel using this method, and, of course, the best deals require flexibility. Just know that the summer months have heavy traffic if you are thinking about going to Europe. And, as always, compare prices. If it's less expensive to fly commercial, then why bother with being a courier? (Unless you just want the adventure.)

Time-Share Vacations

You may have a relative or friend with a time-share located in a great destination that would be great for a honeymoon. Now is not the time to be shy; ask if you can stay at their time-share. There may be minimal maintenance fees, or they may be feeling charitable and let you stay for free. If you're not lucky enough to know someone with a time-share, American Express offers card holders a travel planning and booking service that can lead to large savings on every leg of your travel, and they can book you into a regular time-share vacation because of their extensive network of properties and vacation packages. There are a variety of time-share vacations, so be sure to ask what's available. The following are sample prices for Marriott Vacation Club time-shares (which don't include airfare and ground transportation):

Palm Desert, California: $248 (four days/three nights)
Orlando, Florida: $299 (five days/four nights)
Oahu, Hawaii: $799 (six days/five nights)

(These were the prices as of press time, but you should always check with your travel professional or call ahead for the most current rates.)

Other Ways to Travel
Airline Mileage

If you are a frequent traveler and have accumulated hundreds of thousands of airline miles, you'd better use them before you lose them. What better way to do this than on your honeymoon? If you are just shy of the number of miles you need to fly free, then look into making up the difference by buying the extra air miles. Depending on the airline, you can buy as much as one thousand miles for $100. Ask friends and family if they are willing to donate mileage for your honeymoon airfare.

Hotel Points

Hotel points can help defray the cost of a trip, and when combined with credit card points, like those issued by American Express, you can cash them in or combine the points, whichever is better for your bottom line. Almost every hotel line now has a points system, and many are tied to airline points systems. Go to the Official Airline Guide (www.oag.com) to find out about the three largest alliances (Oneworld, SkyTeam, and Star Alliance). These alliances are made up of airlines such as American Airlines, Continental, United, and others in combination with other partner airlines, and almost all have alliances with hotels and rental companies. If you combine all of these different organizations' point systems with additional points systems offered by credit cards, you can sometimes save a lot of money on travel.

All-Inclusive

One of the best and easiest ways to save money on travel for a honeymoon is to get an all-inclusive package. There are several all-inclusive resorts, including Sandals, Club Med, and Couples. If you are able to get a good deal, you should go for it, because this is a great way to travel. Many of these deals often include excursions and other activities, like water sports or tennis, and they come with American or European meal plans that make everything free and easy. Knowing up front what your costs will be will help you with your honeymoon budget.

You've now gotten a ton of ideas on how to save on your wedding, but there's more. In the next chapter you will find out how to possibly get your entire wedding for free. Curious? Then read on.

Chapter 6

The Beauty of Sponsorship and Bartering

Finding a Sponsor

Bet you didn't think that a little shameless self-promotion could save you money or maybe get the entire cost of your wedding covered, did you? It will involve a little legwork on your part, but you could definitely save some serious cash if you manage to get your wedding sponsored. Not every merchant you approach or consider will be willing to be a sponsor, but those more likely to do so include those just starting out with their businesses or those who are somehow involved in providing products and services that are related, no matter how remotely, to the wedding business. It's not much of a stretch to come up with merchants who are involved in weddings; just think of the hundreds of different types of products and services that you will be using, buying, or renting for your wedding, and you could start by looking there.

From the reception to the honeymoon, there are businesses related to travel, food, wine, hospitality, entertainment, transportation, fashion, jewelry, music, makeup, nails, hair styling, luggage, shoes, clothing, etc., and each of these businesses needs to get their product or service in front of the buying public. Advertising is not always the answer, especially if you are a business just getting started; advertising can be very expensive and is not always a good investment for a fledgling business. What merchants really want is to be able to market directly to their target audience in a way that is easy, inexpensive, and will leave a lasting impression on their potential customers. Oh, and they want those customers to tell their friends and families

about the product or service being marketed. Word of mouth and a positive recommendation trump advertising almost every time.

The reality is that all business owners want to raise their profile and name recognition, and they need to do so by using any means possible—and sponsoring a wedding could give them the creative edge they're looking for. Established businesses tend to already have decent customer bases, so they may not be quite so enthusiastic about your request, but you never know, and it certainly doesn't hurt to ask. Reminder: Before you even think up a list of potential merchants to approach, make sure that you have a lawyer help you draft some kind of agreement that you can use. You

You should always get everything in writing when you are getting a donation or offer of services in exchange for sponsorship.

should always get everything in writing when you are getting a donation or offer of services in exchange for sponsorship. The last thing you want is to arrive at the reception site the day of your wedding to find that your sponsored rental equipment hasn't been delivered and you don't have any chairs, tables, or serving equipment for your reception.

Marketing Your Wedding

You may have a few reservations when it comes to trying to find a merchant to sponsor your wedding. Your first thought is probably, "What if I'm rejected?" I tend to clam up when I have to ask someone for something, too, but keep reading to figure out how to get started, and you'll be saving money in no time. First off, take an assessment of what you will need for your wedding, and target businesses with which you have a connection first. It's always easier to approach someone you know, may have met before, or share a mutual friend in common with. Use the six degrees of separation theory: talk to friends, or the friend of a friend, your dad's golf buddy, the dog walker, the college buddy—whomever and wherever. When it comes time to approach merchants, there are several tacks you could take. One that might be more comfortable if you are making a cold call is to send a letter requesting their sponsorship.

To help get you started, the following is a sample letter that you can use to approach bakeries, florists, DJs, photographers, caterers, reception halls, bridal boutiques, or anyplace else that you think would be interested in sponsoring your wedding. Be sure that you find out whom to address the letter to and get the person's correct name and title. Now is not the time for misspelled words or names. How would you feel if someone was approaching you for money and didn't take the time find out if you were a man or a woman, spelled your name wrong, and sent a letter filled with typos? Not very impressive, right?

Now that you have this template, you can use it for your other letters— just be sure to tailor the personal details to suit your situation and change the name, company, and address each time. But do yourself a favor: Before you lick the envelopes for any of the letters, get someone to check them for style, grammar, and typos. Once you've sent them out, wait about ten days for a

[Date]
[Name]
[Name of business]
[Address]

Dear Mr./Mrs./Ms. [Name]:

I am writing to request your restaurant's sponsorship of my wedding. This is a special time for my fiancé and me, and we want to share it with family and friends, but unfortunately we will not be able to cover all the expenses necessary to make our dreams come true. My parents had their wedding reception at your restaurant, and I would like to continue the tradition.

In my current position as a buyer for Jameson Marketing, I have helped many businesses grow their sales base on average by over 85 percent—and I can help do the same for your business.

We expect to have [number] guests at our reception. I believe that the demographic of our wedding guests is precisely the target market that fits your business. Once they taste your delicious food, I am confident that they would become new customers.

I hope that you will consider this excellent opportunity, and I will follow up with a phone call next week. Thank you in advance for your time and consideration.

Sincerely yours,
[Name]

response. After five days you can be pretty certain that they have received the letter, and you can now make a follow-up call. If you call too soon after the letter is mailed out, you risk coming across as either too pushy or not very business savvy, and that is not the impression you want to make.

Once you are sure they have gotten the letter and had a chance to review it, you can call and ask them if they are interested in accepting your request. If they say no, don't push. Politely thank them for their time and move on to the next person. If they say yes, then you need to thank them, get the details of what they want to provide (the amount of goods, the market value, etc.), and how they want to be mentioned in the program (or whatever method you planned to use to promote their company and name). Before you count on them to deliver on their promise, get a signed written agreement that spells out what each of you will be doing for the other. Then you can move on to the next person.

When you are coming up with your list of potential sponsors to approach, don't just do it by yourself. Ask your friends, family members, and coworkers to think of business owners they know who might be interested. The more ideas you have, the better your chances are of finding sponsors. And don't limit yourself; letters are not the only method you can use to approach prospective sponsors.

Another way is to get a family member or friend to personally introduce you to merchants they know who might be interested in sponsoring your wedding. This does two things: first, it makes it easier for you to bring up the subject with a potential sponsor because it will not be a cold call when you first speak to them, and second, since you have been introduced to the potential sponsor by a mutual friend, it will be harder for them to turn you down. One of the first rules of sales is that it is always harder for someone to say no to a person whom they have met and know, no matter how cursory the acquaintance may be.

You should also approach merchants for sponsorship when you are doing your regular shopping and errands. For example, when you are picking up your dry cleaning, see if your dry cleaner would be interested in sponsoring the dry cleaning of the tablecloths for the reception or pressing your wedding gown and the other attendants' garments. Or if you and the bridesmaids are all getting your hair and makeup done by the same salon, ask them to be a sponsor. Be creative and resourceful about how and where to find sponsors. Remember how Star Jones famously got her entire expensive wedding paid for through sponsorship? She may have been a celebrity, but the concept is the same. Just like she did, you can get all or at least a large portion of the wedding covered this way. When Star Jones did this, she got major corporations to pay for the invitations; wedding attendants' garments; her gown, veil, shoes, and jewelry; and even her honeymoon.

Another way to find potential sponsors is online through many of the B2B (Business to Business) networks that you can join for free, like BreezeWorld.tv, B2BNetwork.us, and FreeB2B.com. If you or anyone in your family belongs to the local chamber of commerce, rotary club, or other similar organization, that could be a good way to find businesses to approach as well.

You may feel uncomfortable approaching your vendors in person at first, but you will get used to doing it after your first few times. To help make the process a little easier, here are some step-by-step tips for a forty- to sixty-second pitch:

1. Develop an early nonverbal connection (eye contact, have good posture, smile, etc.).

2. Speak clearly and get your point across. The first moments of connecting with the vendor are very important. Proper communication lets the vendor know you are serious.

3. Make the pitch: be humble and have a compelling story about your wedding.

4. Discuss why you feel their sponsorship is important (you had your first date there; it has always been a place where your family got together for dinner). You only have a few moments to capture their attention and get your point across.

5. Tell the vendor what is in it for them, which is a fair question since they will be providing the service. Put yourself in their shoes;

what would the benefit to them be? What makes your wedding special? How will your wedding increase the vendor's customers?

6. Ask for the sponsorship.

7. Follow up with a thank-you card.

Media Coverage

In this era of information overload and public access via the Internet, TV, cell phones, YouTube, etc., we have all become accustomed to seeing video and still images aired everywhere. Nothing is more important than having your wedding properly preserved for posterity, but video and still photography can be very expensive, and if it's not done well, it will ruin your keepsakes of the day forever. So if you would like to have video and photography done at either little or no cost, consider getting a media company to cover your wedding. You will certainly know that your chances of getting great pictures are more likely than if your cousin Donny took the pictures. The shots may or may not look like fashion shots, but there are some excellent still, video, and film shooters out there who can really capture wonderful candid moments on film. If for some reason you feel the need to be the center of attention on a larger scale, you can contact television media companies to cover your wedding as a special-interest story for the local affiliate.

On the next page is a sample letter you can use when approaching media types.

What I hope that you learn from what I have highlighted about sponsorships is that there isn't any harm in asking a merchant to sponsor your beautiful event. After all, the worst that can happen is that they say no. While we all hate rejection, even if you try a few times and still don't land a full sponsor, you may just walk away with a couple of great discounts on flower arrangements or specialty boxes of chocolates for your guests' tables. Good luck!

[Date]
[Name]
[Business name]
[Address]

Dear Mr./Mrs./Ms. [Name]:

On Independence Day I am getting married in San Francisco, California, and I have a local-interest story to pitch you. As recent graduates, my fiancé and I are a young couple with a new mortgage, so money is tight, but I have found ways to pay for my wedding by seeking sponsors. I am seeking videography and still photography from you, and in exchange, I am offering marketing services and free publicity. Through my position as a marketing advertising executive, I have many contacts at top firms with whom I can help market your business, if you are interested.

Our wedding ceremony is being held at the Mountain Top Hotel, an excellent venue with tons of opportunities for valuable shots for print and television. This would be a great opportunity for you to showcase your business, meet other potential clients, and to demonstrate your company's kindness. Our guests are also the perfect demographic that will suit your business.

Thank you for your consideration. Please give me a call at 555-5555 if you have questions.

Sincerely yours,
[Name]

Bartering Tips

Planning a wedding in a bad economy is never fun, and this is especially true now. However, there is one definite advantage—people are hurting for business, so they are more inclined to make deals and haggle over pricing. This is especially true with people who provide services like hair styling, makeup, and catering. If you are not good at negotiating or haggling with vendors, find someone who is, or develop your confidence by starting with smaller, less important items.

If you are the kind of person who doesn't do well at flea markets because you can't bargain, then you need to practice—a lot. Bartering is not so scary if you realize that it has been around since time began, and if you have a skill that is in high demand or are willing to work your fanny off, you can make the wedding of your dreams become a reality. So let's talk about what bartering is. The definition of bartering is the exchange of goods and services for other goods and services. If you have a special skill or job experience—for example, a chef, carpenter, or Web site designer—then you could use that skill to barter for either price reductions or exact exchanges with vendors.

To help you do this, there is a Web site devoted to brides and grooms who want to take this route. It's called BigDayBarter.com, and it acts much like a matchmaking service: Couples post services or products that they can offer businesses, and businesses can go to the site and see if there are things that they need or want to barter for in exchange. Some of the kinds of barters that have occurred have included a couple who completed a "honey do" list for a church in exchange for a free ceremony site, a couple who cleaned up after catering functions in exchange for catering, and a professional videographer who did some promo shots for a reception venue in exchange for a reception site. If you think that you don't have anything you can barter with, just offer to work for free for some of the vendors and see if they are interested. You could do housekeeping, wash cars, run errands, take a pet to the vet, do yard work, etc.

Ask friends or family first about bartering, because they may be part of a bartering group or club or know of one. Bartering has become hugely popular because of the economy and the need for good quality services. Depending on what you are looking for, someone might just be able to exchange the very service you need.

If you do not feel comfortable asking friends and family to barter with, you can try Web sites such as Craigslist.org, UExchange.com, and InternationalBarterExchange.net. Make sure that the person you are bartering with agrees on what your barter exchange includes. For example, if you are going to cook dinner for a wedding photographer who, in exchange, is going to shoot your wedding, be very clear about what shots he/she will get, how long he/she will work, who will pay for film, and so on. Conversely, make sure that you are both clear about the service you are providing. As always, make sure you have the details in writing.

When you take stock of all of the things that you have done to save for, and on, your wedding, I hope that you will be able to say with confidence that you did what you could to stay solvent, stick to your budget, and lay the foundation for the long, happy life you will have with your future husband. The practical tips and resources I have given thus far in this book are pretty obvious once you start thinking like a saver and not a spender. In the next chapter, however, I will discuss some aspects of the wedding that will not only save you money, time, and effort, but, more importantly, will speak to your values. The money savings from some of these suggestions might not be readily apparent at first, but they are tips that can also reveal your inner beauty. Read on to find out how to have a green, sustainable wedding and how to use technology to accomplish that goal and save time and money.

Chapter 7

The Ecotechno Wedding

With the public's acceptance of the science behind global warming in recent years, the environmental movement has become an integral part of our culture. The green movement and sustainable living are no longer a fad, and even cable networks have entire channels devoted to green living, building, and so on. So it's only natural that the green movement would spill over into the wedding industry. As we raise our level of awareness about how much our carbon footprint has changed the planet, more people are trying to change how they live and work in order to minimize their impact on the environment.

More and more brides and grooms are looking for ecofriendly or green ways of doing things, not just as a choice that they embrace when the mood strikes, but as a way of life. They want to make a statement about their values and make a difference on a daily basis. But what does green or ecofriendly mean? Being green is really nothing more than being environmentally conscious of your impact on the fragile ecosystems around you and on the earth. It means limiting the amount of trash you create, scaling back how much vital nonrenewable resources you use, reusing or recycling as much as you can in your daily life, and expecting the same from industrial and commercial enterprises.

The goal is to minimize your impact on the world around you by making environmentally positive decisions about everything—from the car you drive, to the clothes you wear, to the food you eat, to how much trash you generate, to what kind of energy you use and how much energy you can save. This philosophy views lifestyle choices as a way to make dramatic changes that improve the environment for everyone, not just those who can afford to or who have the freedom to speak up without fear of reprisal.

One way to minimize your impact on the planet is to get away from paper for invitations, announcements, wedding books, pictures, etc. by doing as much as possible online. But the Internet is much more than just a way to save paper. It is a powerful conduit for communicating ideas, sharing thoughts, shopping, you name it. Most everything can be done more quickly, cheaply, and easily via the World Wide Web. In the old days, if you asked someone how to find a local bridal store or tuxedo store they told you to look it up in the yellow pages. You'd then have to call the store and make an appointment to go down and check it out. Now you can do a Google search and go right to the shop's Web site, see what products are offered, view pictures, see how much things cost, find out about the store's return policies, etc. and do it without ever putting gas in your tank or leaving the comfort of your home.

We now take this ease of use, speed, and low cost for granted and there is a seemingly unlimited range of ways the Internet can help make planning your wedding less stressful. You can now use the Web to create your own wedding Web site complete with photo galleries, ways for people to buy your gifts directly from your bridal registry, and updates on all of your pre-wedding planning. You can also use the web to keep track of your thoughts in an online journal or as part of a blog. The Internet is so much a part of how we resource or research things nowadays it's a wonder how we ever got anything done before.

The Ecofriendly Wedding

Here are some of the elements of weddings that are being made green: the engagement ring, wedding bands, and jewelry; the location of the ceremony, reception, and honeymoon; the invitations; the food and drink served; the flowers used for the bridal bouquet, the bouquet toss, and the centerpieces; the favors; and the wedding party's attire. If you want to make a statement about your values but don't want to inconvenience your guests, the following are some ways you can make your wedding greener and save some money.

Rings and Things

Couples choosing to go green and sustainable can now do so from the moment they get engaged. By choosing an engagement ring, wedding bands, and other jewelry that are ecologically and morally responsible, the couple can put their values front and center. The diamonds that you may have your heart set on for your engagement ring and wedding band and the gold that it is set in both may symbolize love and eternity, but in reality these precious gems and ores could be the cause of pain and suffering across the globe and hurt the environment as well. If you want your jewelry to be green, you can do the right thing by refusing to have "blood diamonds" and newly mined gold be a part of your jewelry choices. You may have heard of the term *blood diamonds* from the movie *Blood Diamond* starring Leonardo DiCaprio, but what are they?

Blood diamonds, or what the UN refers to as "conflict diamonds," are diamonds mined in war-torn countries in Africa by violent rebels bent on gaining control of the country. These rebels often brutally abuse the human rights of the local people enslaved to mine the diamonds and kill innocent victims in their quest for this valuable commodity. The sale of these diamonds helps fund insurgencies, illegal armies to invade surrounding countries, or rebels' regimes and atrocities.

This cross-border violence has made diamond-mining countries and their neighbors in Africa vulnerable and has politically destabilized the region, especially in Sierra Leone, Liberia, and Angola. But not all African countries that mine for diamonds practice or condone these kinds of abuses. In countries like Botswana and Namibia, the government protects the human rights of mine workers, makes sure they get a livable wage, stops the severe degradation of the environment caused by destructive mining practices, and keeps rebels and other criminals from co-opting the diamond trade. The Botswana and Namibian governments' efforts have paid off, and their standards of living are now much higher than others in the region, and the people have been able to see their countries' futures improve.

To play a part in stopping conflict diamonds from entering the marketplace, you can shop for diamonds at jewelers who are registered with an organization called StopBloodDiamonds.org. This Web site has a directory of retail jewelers (online and brick and mortar) who have registered and provided proof that they don't buy conflict diamonds. You can also go to Web sites like BrilliantEarth.com, LeberJewelry.com, and JamesAllen.com to purchase diamonds and jewelry that is certified conflict-free, but you should do your homework and ask your local jeweler about the provenance of their diamonds, too. If they can't tell you where their diamonds came from, guarantee that their diamonds and other gems are not blood diamonds, or show you their System of Warranties statements, then they are not reputable, and you should shop elsewhere. To see what one of these statements looks like and learn more about them, go to DiamondFacts.org.

Green Gold

In addition to not buying blood diamonds, couples can help the environment by choosing to wear jewelry that was not made with newly mined gold. The process for mining and extracting gold from the environment endangers and destroys precious, vulnerable ecosystems, and just as with diamonds, it often results in the enslavement or indentured servitude of the local populations. In most cases, the local people have few options for good jobs and are often forced to work for little or no pay in dangerous, toxic conditions.

The method for removing gold from the earth involves the use of toxic chemicals, like mercury or cyanide, to separate the gold fragments from rock, soil, and other ores. In the case of cyanide, the surrounding rock is crushed, a cyanide solution is poured over the rock and gold, and then the mixture is sluiced until the gold is left behind. This process leaves behind millions of tons of toxic leftover sludge that ends up in rivers and groundwater where the local people get their drinking water. This sludge contains cyanide, cadmium, mercury, and lead, and as it flows through the various lakes, streams, rivers, and oceans, it eventually ends up polluting water sources around the world and contaminating fish.

There are safe, socially responsible alternatives to using new gold, however. It is now fairly easy to buy conflict-free, environmentally sustainable gold from jewelers that use postconsumer (recycled) gold. Some of the better-known companies are PreciousEarthJewelry.com, GreenKarat.com, and EthicalMetalsmiths.org. Another option, if you want to go green rather than gold, is to do your own recycling and wear a family heirloom, or you could have some of your old jewelry melted down to create signature pieces for you and your groom. Experts estimate that there is enough gold in old jewelry that is sitting in safety deposit boxes and jewelry boxes to keep the gold supply going for at least the next thirty years, making the mining of new gold unnecessary. If you really want to embrace the ecofriendly ethic, you could eliminate buying jewelry altogether and instead rent your jewelry from a service like BorrowedBling.com, AdornBrides.com, or Avelle (www .bagborroworsteal.com).

To Paper or Not to Paper, That Is the Question

If you want to set the tone of your ecofriendly wedding, you can do so by eliminating paper products entirely on your big day, using only nontoxic ink on 100 percent postconsumer (recycled) paper, or using paper made from products that are renewable or sustainable. If you think this won't save much paper or that it won't make much of a difference, here are some of the things you will buy for your wedding that are made with paper:

- Engagement announcements

- Save the date cards

- Shower invitations

- Shower thank-you notes

- Wedding invitations

- Ceremony programs

- Table numbers

- Place cards

- Menu cards

- Wedding announcements

- Wedding thank-you notes

- Personal notes

There are dozens of paper sources that specialize in either recycled or tree-free papers. You can even get custom paper hand made from the same flowers that will be featured in your wedding at Of the Earth's Web site, www.custompaper.com. To find quality recycled paper, some Web sites to look for include TwistedLimbPaper.com, ConsciousCreative.com, Festivale .net, and TashaRaeDesigns.com.

To find sources for non-tree-harvested papers, GreenFieldPaper.com, InviteSite.com, and EarthlyAffair.com are good places to start. If you want a directory of places to find tree-free paper, RainForestWeb.org has a good list that you can use. Or you could save money and go paper-free, instead using an online product like Evite.com to e-mail all of your wedding correspondence. Instead of paper place cards, you could use leaves, rocks, nuts, or other natural products.

Location Matters

The location of the ceremony and reception is another place where couples are choosing to go green, and there are a number of ways to do this, including combining the ceremony and reception in one location to cut down on travel and transportation and choosing venues that provide a natural setting and give back to the planet somehow, like nature preserves and parks. Couples are also looking at venues closer to home to eliminate the need for a lot of long-distance travel and seeking out venues that practice sustainability (such as organic restaurants), recycle, use green products, and use clean, renewable energy sources.

One option is to have your ceremony and reception at a green hotel. Not only will the wedding venue be green, but out-of-town guests can stay in green accommodations. To be considered green, a hotel must practice sustainable living and have rooms that are furnished and decorated with recycled, organic, or sustainable materials. To find a green hotel, go to the Green Hotel Association's Web site, www.greenhotels.com, which has a listing by state and specifies which hotels have achieved Green Seal certification standards.

Also see if your hotel or venue is LEED (Leadership in Environmental and Energy Design) certified by the U.S. Green Building Council or has been certified as an EnergyStar (energy efficient, just like on appliances) location. If a hotel has either of these certifications, it means they use green building materials and sustainable products and have energy-efficient appliances. What is great about LEED venues is that they have practices in place to save on water consumption, don't use toxic cleaning chemicals, recycle, and encourage guests to save on water and pollution by limiting the frequency of sheet and towel changes.

Churches and historic buildings offer another chance to go green; because of their architectural beauty, they are already decorated and don't require a lot of extra products to improve their appearance. If the caterer and florist are also earth-friendly and organic, then these can become ready-made green places to host your big day.

Travel and Transportation

Of all the pollutants and damages to the environment, few can compare to the combustion engine. If you want to go green, one area that you can definitely make a difference in is the vehicle you drive or hire, or the distances you travel. As already mentioned, one way to reduce your impact on the environment is to have your ceremony and reception in the same location. This is not only more convenient for caterers, rental companies, and guests, it also means less gas usage.

If you will have out-of-town wedding guests, suggest that they check out GreenYour.com, which has a transporation section that has links and information on some of the airlines' policies on going green. The site also has a list of car-rental agencies that offer hybrids, electric cars, or biofuel vehicles, as well as limousine services that are green.

When looking for a green limousine company, be sure to find out if they have hybrid vehicles, and verify what the vehicle's source of power is and that it is prominently displayed on the car. Some green limo companies are even offering organic snacks in addition to the usual amenities like telephones, TVs, and stereos. Try Eco-Limo.com to hire a green limo for your special event or Bauer's Limo at www.bauerit.com, which offers green corporate transport nationwide. Through these Web sites, you can check the fleet of vehicles, make reservations, compare amenities, and start an account.

Flowers

The choice you make for wedding flowers can have big environmental consequences. Many flowers are imported from developing countries where pesticide use is very high and labor conditions and wages are low. Choosing a florist where organically grown, in-season, local flowers are used can be a much better, earth-friendly choice. This will remove the need for long-distance transportation and reduce your flowers' carbon footprint. To find organic fresh flowers, you can go OrganicBouquet.com, you can buy them at your local farmers' market (to find a farmers' market in your area, go to LocalHarvest.org, where they have a nationwide listing of farmers' markets as well as suppliers of organic produce, flowers, and other products), you can force your own bulbs or grow your own flowers if you are a gardener, or you can use dried flowers or even silk flowers as an alternative. And be sure to reuse your flowers by taking the flowers from the ceremony to decorate the reception venue. After the big day, you can then donate the flowers to a local hospice or hospital and deduct the cost of the donation on your taxes.

Centerpieces

One place where you can really make an impact is by doing something different and meaningful for table centerpieces. Rather than use cut flowers, you could use potted flowers and plants that can later be planted by your guests, or you could make arrangements of greenery picked up in the forest or in your own backyard. Even the vase can be green if you choose to use those made from recycled glass or sustainable products like cork or bamboo, or purchase items from VivaTerra.com, which offers recycled or green decorations and housewares.

RecycledGlassworks.com has wonderful bowls made by artist Lauren Becker, and everything is made with recycled glass. Another place to find artisanal recycled glass items is at Greenfeet.com, which specializes in green living products. They have gorgeous ecospheres—completely enclosed ecosystems—that are sure to be a hit. You could do something really simple like fill a recycled-glass bowl with fresh fruit, locally found greenery, and/or some small potted flowers or plants. At the end of the day, have one of the members of your support team be in charge of handing out the bowls to guests as they depart, or you could donate the leftover fruit to a food bank or homeless shelter, which will be tax deductible.

Bouquet from
Neighbors Garden
with trained
Butterflies.

Favors

One huge source of waste, pollution, and cost at weddings is favors. Brides spend hours trying to think of original ideas that will be appreciated but don't break the bank. As long as you come up with ideas that are organic, and you are mindful that the companies you patronize practice ethical trade and labor practices, you should be fine. Check one of the many organic or ecofriendly Web sites already mentioned for favor ideas; many of those sites sell a range of products that would be suitable. Another site to consider is ChocolateBar.com, which has a line of premium chocolates called Endangered Species. They donate 10 percent of the proceeds from the sales to support "species, habitat and humanity" through the African Wildlife Foundation (www.awf.org), and they buy their all-natural milk and dark chocolate from small farmers in Nigeria who receive a fair wage. The company also sponsors students, provides scholarships, and has established a co-op. As if that weren't enough to convince you, their Web site is powered by 100 percent solar energy.

One huge source of waste, pollution, and cost at weddings is favors.

If you're interested in flowers and gardening, you could consider giving small trees, plants, or flowers from PlantAMemory.com, which has a wide variety of flower-bulb wedding favors and seeds in many design and color options. SeedsofChange.com has a huge list of organic and heirloom seeds that are rare and wonderful, or you can go to SeedSavers.org for rare heirloom seeds. The Tender Seed Company (www.favorswithseeds.com) has money-saving and seed-shaped favors that you can plant later, as well as DIY projects.

The National Arbor Day Foundation (www.arborday.org) will become your new best source for gift ideas, because their trees come delivered in a recyclable plastic tube, and the label can be customized. GreenWorldProject.net provides live evergreen tree seedling favors, and their motto is, "By giving trees or seeds to your guests, everlasting memories will take root and grow along with your marriage."

One of the best ideas comes from the I Do Foundation's (www.idofoundation.org) Favors for Charity program, which allows you to make tax-deductible donations to your favorite charity in honor of your guests in lieu of favors. Once you sign up, you can choose from a list of nonprofit organizations.

Food and Drink

Your caterer should practice organic and sustainable sourcing by buying from local organic suppliers of meat, seafood, and produce. If wine and coffee will be served, you should try to find fair trade organic suppliers and see about using recycled glassware. To find fair trade organic wine and coffee, go to OrganicWineTrade Company.com, Luxist.com (which has a list of top ten fair trade wines), and Green America (www.coopamerica.org). MotherEarthCoffee.com and GroundsForChange.com both can help you find the right coffee to serve.

Wedding-Party Attire

One of the most important decisions a bride has to make is choosing the kind of dress she will wear. It used to be that wedding dresses came in two price categories—expensive and inexpensive—with little in between, ranging from hand-made, one-of-a-kind designer dresses running in the thousands and tens of thousands of dollars to off-the-rack dresses that usually needed to be altered to fit and look more customized. But this is no longer the case. Consumer demand, the power of the wedding industry to impact what designers offer each season, and the recognition of the fashion industry that the more women who get to have the dress of their dreams—no matter what their size or budget—the more money they make, have changed this. Thankfully, no matter what your budget, the wedding gown industry is offering more and more conscientious fashion options.

In line with this response to consumer demand is the latest trend—ecofriendly wedding-party clothes. Green brides, grooms, and attendants can wear wedding attire made with organic fabrics, or buy fabrics made with natural products that were grown sustainably (no child labor or workers subjected to harsh living conditions and poor wages) and then produced in sustainable factories. Another way to be responsible to is to buy a vintage used gown, rent a gown, make a gown with recycled fabric, or wear your mother's dress. This option can save a lot of money, too.

Web sites to check out include BridesAgainstBreastCancer.com, where you can purchase a once-worn or sample gown, and the proceeds help women with breast cancer. Other online options for used bridal gowns include eBay.com, TheDressmarket.net, WeddingDressMarket.com, and BravoBride.com. EncoreBridal.com sells preowned couture wedding dresses and bridal accessories and is dedicated to reusing wedding gowns and other accoutrements because it eliminates or reduces waste and the impact on the environment. It's also a green business that uses recycled paper for stationery, uses biodegradable shipping products, and maximizes fuel efficiency in its transportation.

If having a new dress is important to you, consider earth-friendly fabrics such as hemp, organic cotton, linen, Tencel, and silk. You can check out the ecofriendly-fabric options for wedding gowns at OrganicWedding .com (swatches are available), GetConscious.com, PristinePlanet.com, and ThreadheadCreations.com. When the big day is over, consider donating your wedding dress to a charitable organization, which is the ultimate in recycling and is tax deductible, too. Some organizations to consider are the aforementioned BridesAgainstBreastCancer.com; the I Do Foundation (www.idofoundation.org), which will donate 20 percent of the proceeds from the sale of your dress to the charity of your choice; and the GlassSlipperProject.org, a program that distributes bridesmaids' dresses and other formal dresses to high school students unable to afford prom attire.

If having a new dress is important to you, consider earth-friendly fabrics such as hemp, organic cotton, linen, Tencel, and silk.

Honeymoon

Whether you choose to stay in a green hotel, go local to save on fuel, or go on an ecotour, there are many ways your honeymoon can be green. The most important thing is to find ecofriendly tour or travel operators. A great place to start is GreenYour.com, a great resource for all kinds of green travel-related things. In addition, check out EcoTrotters.com for ecofriendly resort information or GreatGreenWeddings.com for ecofriendly honeymoon ideas.

Your Wedding and the Internet

Whether you are researching vendors and venues for your wedding or are sending out electronic save-the-date announcements, few resources are as cost-effective, easy to use, fast, and useful as the Internet. In today's world of blogging, social networking, and informational Web sites, there are literally unlimited resources at your fingertips, and much of it is free. Just Google "wedding," and millions of results are listed, including wedding directories such as BestWeddingSites.com, which lists wedding-related Web sites. There are also portals that are clearinghouses of information on everything related to weddings: sites and blogs devoted to the planning and organizing aspects of your wedding, directories of vendors, local bridal sites and blogs, interactive calendars, interactive budgets, budgeting how-to's,

As more and more people become accustomed to using Internet-based products and services, the role of the Internet in wedding planning will grow even larger.

worksheets, social networks—you get the picture. Some of the biggest, most comprehensive, and widely used portals include Bride.com, Brides.com, WeddingChannel .com, and WeddingWire.com. There are even Web sites that help you create your own wedding Web site quickly and easily, and for free. Some of the best include eWedding.com, MyWedding.com, YourWeddingPlace.com, Momentville.com, TheKnot.com, WeddingChannel.com and many others.

As more and more people become accustomed to using Internet-based products and services, the role of the Internet in wedding planning will grow even larger. In this section I'll give you many recommendations for user-friendly and well-organized sites and blogs.

Your Wedding Web Site or Blog

Many of us now use the Internet for just about everything, from paying bills to shopping, and even connecting with friends. Although it may not be for everyone, creating a blog or Web site can be a great way to share photographs, send out invitations, share your thoughts about the wedding-planning process, keep in touch with friends and family, give your guests access to your registries, and give vendors a feeling for your sense of style and who you are as a couple. Web sites like SharedWeddings.com, OurBrideSpace.com, and others previously mentioned let you create a free Web site that you can customize to fit your style, and many of these sites come with a blogging component.

When we discussed the planning process earlier in the book, I mentioned some of the tools and things you would need to be organized, including your wedding book. If you use your wedding Web site wisely, it could be an important addition to your list of tools or even replace your wedding book entirely. Depending on how user friendly and chock-full of tools it is, your Web site can become an integral part of your support team. Think of it as the perfect assistant: It never gets tired or cranky, it doesn't argue with you about your choices, it gets along with the other members of your wedding party, it doesn't get drunk at the reception and fall into the chocolate fountain, it can get many jobs done at once and in a short amount of time, and it can keep you in touch with guests, vendors, and others no matter how far away you are. Oh, did I mention that it is free? This is an important consideration since we are trying to save money, not just time.

Whether you are inclined to share your wedding plans with the world or just your family, friends, and guests, your site can be as public or as private as you choose. You have the option to require visitors to submit a password before they can access the site, which can help keep spammers at bay, prevent just anyone from leaving a comment or viewing your personal photos and thoughts, and act as a central message center to keep certain communications private.

If you are still not convinced, the following are some of the benefits of having your own Web site:

- **Guest information.** Your wedding Web site can be an information clearinghouse and keep you from having to deal with seemingly hundreds of phone calls regarding the details of the ceremony and reception. It can be a one-stop resource for things like the address of the church, temple, or mosque; time and date of the rehearsal dinner, ceremony, and reception; and directions and maps for all the wedding activities. If you are inviting kids, include kid-friendly details about the hotel (e.g., babysitting, crib rental) and the area (e.g., local play areas, nearest Toys "R" Us).

- **Vendor information.** If guests are interested in wedding details such as the venue and the food, you can include links to your vendors' Web sites. (Plus, you can offer to advertise your vendors on your site for free as part of what you offer if you approach them to be sponsors.) You can also direct vendors to your site to get a feel for who you are. Download sample pictures of your style and ideas (for the ceremony and reception, your dress and bridesmaids' dresses, and colors) that you can share with vendors.

- **Photos and videos.** One of the more fun and interesting aspects of wedding sites is the ability to host and edit photos, create animated scrapbooks and albums, and even create your own movies from either stills or video. Some of the best online products to help you edit your images, put them into albums (complete with music and scrapbooking tools), and share them with others include SmileBox .com, Flickr.com, Picknik.com, and PhotoScape.com. And if you insist on printing out your photos, places like Costco and Sam's Club let you develop prints and save your images on a CD that you can edit later.

- **Invites and RSVPs.** If you aren't using an online invitation service like Evite.com, MyPunchBowl.com, or EZ Invitations from Freeze .com, many sites have components for handling invitations and tracking RSVPs, special meals, and menu selections.

- **Tools.** Tools such as budget databases, budget worksheets, checklists, wedding books, time lines, seating charts, cost calculators, menu planners, drink calculators, and many other options are often part of the package and can be real time and money savers. The trend toward cell phone optimization of Web sites and blogs has now made it possible for your friends, family, and service providers to exchange information via your cell phone or PDA.

- **Personal details.** Just as businesses have "about" pages that include information on key staffers, your Web page can introduce people to you, your fiancé, and your wedding party. On these pages you can detail how you and your fiancé met, how he proposed to you, and what a great shower your maid of honor put together for you.

- **Registries.** Nothing beats the Internet today when it comes to shopping. If you have set up registries for wedding gifts or your honeymoon, having a dedicated page for your registries and providing links to stores makes it easy for your guests. In many cases they can purchase gifts right from the link in your Web site without ever having to leave home. This can be particularly helpful if you live far away from friends and family.

- **Event calendars and notifications.** You can include a calendar of events for your wedding activities, including engagement parties, wedding showers, bachelor/bachelorette parties, and rehearsal dinners, and you can send out a group e-mail directing your guests to your Web site when it's been changed or updated.

- **Wedding-party information.** This includes checklists and details for your maid of honor, best man, bridesmaids, and groomsmen.

One downside to relying on the Internet is that those who may not be Internet or tech savvy, or don't have computer access, might not be able to enjoy your Web site. You can keep these people in the loop by sending out the equivalent of a "Christmas letter" that details all of the preparations and plans, including contact and event information.

If you prefer to have a stand-alone blog, some of the best free blogging platforms available include WordPress.com, SixApart.com, and Blogger .com. The benefit of these is that you don't have to know anything about coding or design, they have dozens of templates and design schemes (including some just for girls, brides, and weddings) to choose from, and they can get you started in just a few minutes' time. You don't need to have any technical skills whatsoever to create a blog, and they are free.

Social Networking

Early forms of social networking included communicating using two cans connected by a string or talking with your neighbor at your fence—but we have come a long way since then. Now we communicate through such technologies as texting, blogs, and what is called social media. These new technologies have changed the way we communicate. Now you can chat, text, and tweet live with anyone in the world instantaneously on the Web and have the feeds go directly to your cell phone, too. And if you already have a blog, you can link it to your social media accounts. Some of the more popular social networks include Twitter.com, Facebook.com, MySpace .com, and two social networks devoted just to weddings, NearlyWeds.com, and TheKnot.com. Using social networking to connect with your guests and bridal party can be a godsend if you choose not to set up a Web site or blog, or it can be used in conjunction with those. These may seem intrusive to some, but they can give you a quick, easy, free line of communication that can help keep everyone in the loop during the planning process. They are also handy for sharing photos and videos, planning showers, letting people know about upcoming parties and activities, and providing links to your online registries, and most have a blog component that you can use like a diary, a wonderful keepsake and source of memories later on.

Online Internet Faxing

If you are having a wedding out of town and need to be able to e-mail vendor contracts back and forth, you should consider using an online faxing service. Online faxing works in this way: The Internet faxing company assigns you a number depending on your area or gives you an 800 number, and this fax number is tied to your e-mail account. When you receive a fax, it will go to your e-mail account, and in addition you will also be able to send PDF files, TIFF files, and Word documents. There are several online faxing companies, such as Efax.com, MyFax.com, and MetroHighSpeed .com. Most have thirty-day free trials, monthly fees vary from $9.95 to $16.95, and fax storage ranges from thirty days to unlimited. This type of service makes it easy to fax without having to deal with a cumbersome fax dial-up, it helps you to keep track of your contracts, and it reduces the need for paper, thus saving the environment.

You have successfully set up your budget, secured your sponsors, and researched ecofriendly wedding options, and you've just finished your Web site. Now how do you pull together all the pieces of this huge puzzle? The most important people you will be spending time over the next year will most likely be those you count on the most—your support team. To find out who these people are and what they can and can't be expected to do, see the pages that follow.

Chapter 8

Your Core Support Team

Let's take a moment for a big group hug. By now we all recognize that orchestrating a wedding ceremony, reception, and honeymoon without a hitch is going to take some doing. For things to go smoothly, it will take a team effort to pull all of the pieces together. You will need the support of family, friends, a wedding planner (if you go that route), professional vendors, and the alignment of the stars. That's the logistics side of things. What is often overlooked is how much emotional support it will take. Weddings bring out all sorts of emotions in everyone (as you're probably experiencing now). You are transitioning from being single to being a wife, and that can be very stressful. Your groom is going from being single to being married. Your parents are losing their "little girl," and his parents are watching their son form a new life and family.

With a wedding to plan, you have a very short amount of time to sort out all your emotions and anxieties, so staying sane through all of this will be a challenge. Be prepared to get opinions (solicited or not) from most everyone you encounter. You will have people telling you what you should and shouldn't do and how you should and shouldn't spend your money. But if you have a team of supporters behind you, it won't be hard to weather whatever anyone doles out. Make sure that you really consider who it is you want to be part of your team. You want people around you who can handle crises well, who don't crack under pressure, who are reliable and true to their word, and who will stand up for you when you can't do it yourself. So let's take a look at who you want on your team.

Be prepared to get opinions (solicited or not) from most everyone you encounter.

Your Hubby-To-Be

Your partner will more than likely be a little confused by the role he's supposed to play. Try not to exclude him, and find out how much or how little he wants to be involved in the planning process. You may have to guide him as to what role he can play and what he can or should be responsible for, but this guidance will pay off later. Let's be honest; the reality is that in most cases the groom would rather be out fishing, golfing, or watching a game on TV than sitting down to discuss swatches, color schemes, and invitations—but don't assume anything. Your guy might just want to play a larger role in the planning.

As I outlined in the Bride's Checklist in chapter 2, the time to find out how much or how little the groom will be doing is the moment you both sit down to begin your preliminary planning. The last thing you want is to find out midstream that you are out there on your own. If either party feels left out, taken advantage of, or resents the other party for slacking off, you will have the makings of an explosive situation. Neither one of you should be forced to do more than you are comfortable with or capable of doing—which is why deciding on and agreeing to the division of labor from the outset is so important.

If you were honest with each other when you initially discussed your expectations of the roles and responsibilities each of you would play, then you should be able to work together as a team. The additional support you will receive from the other members of your team should balance out the workload so that no one is overly burdened. What is important is to understand your groom's strengths and weaknesses, and skills and talents, and match them to the tasks at hand (this is true of all of your team members). It's actually pretty easy to do this if you take a look at the examples that follow.

- If your groom is a CPA, is good at numbers, and likes to manage money (and is good at it), he might be a good candidate for helping with or managing the finances and budget.

- If your groom is organized, detail oriented, and good at project management, then maybe he would like to be the one who is in charge of putting together your time line, making the checklists, and keeping the planning process on target and organized.

- If your groom is wild about planes, trains, and automobiles, then maybe he would like to be the one in charge of arranging for the limousine transportation to and from the ceremony, reception, and honeymoon.

- If your groom is in the marketing business, then he might be better suited to signing up sponsors and handling the "marketing" side of your wedding planning.

- If he is a people person, maybe he could be the one to smooth the ruffled feathers that invariably crop up when designing the guest lists and seating arrangements.

- If he is a good communicator, he might be the perfect person to coordinate speeches at the rehearsal dinner and/or reception.

- If he is good at following through on tasks and doesn't mind dealing with city hall, then it might be a good idea to let him get the marriage license (unless your particular state law requires both of you to be present) or find the officiant for your wedding.

For additional ideas about how to involve the groom or for ways to make the groom feel more included, some informative Web sites include GroomsAdvice.com, GroomsOnline.com, and BrideandGroom.com.

Your Parents

This is also your parents' big day. They get to brag to all their friends that you are getting married, and if they are footing the bill, they also get to brag about how much it is going to cost. I know that it's sometimes hard not to butt heads and that you wish your parents would treat you more like

an adult, but don't deny them bragging rights. If you understand that what they are really trying to say is that they are proud of you and want you to be happy, then maybe, just maybe, you won't get under each other's skin. One way to help prevent friction is to clearly define each set of parents' roles and responsibilities right from the start. If you can get them to feel like they are doing more than just writing a check or showing up like any other guest, then chances are there will be less tension. Make sure that each parent feels like he or she has a part to play so that no one feels left out or slighted.

Just know that you all will have to have a lot of patience with each other. You may all drive each other insane before this all over, but make this phrase your mantra, and you should be able to arrive at your wedding day in one piece: "They only want what's best for me, they only want what's best for me." Got it?

The Guest List: The Second-Biggest Hurdle of Wedding Planning

After the budget, drawing up a list of guests and a seating chart is the wedding task fraught with the most tension. Accept in advance that, even in the best of circumstances, there will most likely be power struggles and dissension about this. The guest list is probably one of the most intensely fought over parts of planning a wedding. For instance, your groom's mother may want to invite her entire book club, while your father couldn't care less who you decide to add to the guest list as long as the reception doesn't cost him an arm and a leg. It's important for you to keep in mind that just because your parents (meaning yours and your groom's) are either paying for the entire wedding or just part of it, they don't have license to invite their law firm's entire client list to the wedding, or their softball league, for that matter. The wedding is, after all, your day to share your declaration of love for each other with those nearest and dearest to you.

The guest list is probably one of the most intensely fought over parts of planning a wedding.

Conversely, you and the groom also shouldn't insist on inviting more guests than you or your parents can afford. One solution might be to come up with a total number of guests based on the budget and then divide the number of guests that can be invited among the two sets of parents and you and your groom (consider 50 percent for you and the groom and 25 percent for each set of parents). However you decide to divide up the guest list, don't let this be the source of hurt feelings, rancor, or stress.

Bridesmaids and Groomsmen

Bridesmaids and groomsmen are probably the greatest assets on your support team, and you should lean on them whenever possible for guidance and emotional support. These are your closest friends, right? Just try to avoid assigning them tasks they either aren't qualified or inclined to do. A good metaphor might be that while they are the nominees for your cabinet, that doesn't mean they will necessarily pass the confirmation hearing. You are bringing together a bunch of people for a common cause, but that doesn't mean that everyone is going to get along. Within your cabinet there will be many different personalities. Some of your friends and wedding attendants may be strangers, while some may have a history—for good or ill. For example, your two best friends from grade school, Jill and Maddy, may still be mad at each other because Maddy stole Jill's boyfriend in the fifth grade. Seriously, these kinds of clashes can erupt and cause problems for everyone if not managed properly. Be aware of the group dynamic, and try to assess if the people you have chosen for your support team will be able to get along with each other.

Also, be clever when matching your bridal party with various tasks. Know what each member's strengths are and assign the tasks accordingly. For example, don't give Jan, your maid of honor, the task of planning your shower if she cracks under pressure and has drama-queen tendencies. Maybe Jan is the queen of finding bargains and is a shopping diva, however, and if that's the case, then have her help you get the best prices on things like the wedding gown and wedding favors. Know who you can count on to be responsible and accountable and who your "worker bees" are in the group.

The same goes for the groomsmen. Your fiancé should know who his go-to guy is so that when the morning of the wedding comes, you know that your fiancé will arrive for the ceremony on time.

The better you are at delegating jobs to your support team, the less you and the groom will have to bear on your own. If you still feel like you need more help, then now is the time to look into finding a wedding consultant.

The better you are at delegating jobs to your support team, the less you and the groom will have to bear on your own.

Working with a Wedding Consultant

Trying to juggle work, family obligations, and all of the time-consuming tasks of planning a wedding can overwhelm even the most organized bride. Before you even meet with a wedding planner, you should know exactly how much or how little you will want him to be responsible for and what kind of communication methods you prefer. For example, if you have the kind of job that involves a lot of meetings, phone calls, e-mails, and time on the road, you may prefer to talk on the phone or e-mail after work hours at home. It doesn't matter what method of communication you choose; all that matters is that you are clear about your expectations about how and how often you will be in contact.

For an event as costly and emotion-packed as your wedding, it's essential that you get recommendations for wedding planners from your friends and family. Nothing is better than word of mouth. Ask people whom they have used in the past and to be honest about the wedding planner's management style, the pros and cons of the experience, and whether or not they would hire that planner again. If getting a recommendation is not an option, go to the Association of Certified Professional Wedding Consultants's Web site, www.acpwc.com, and find one by searching their list of members.

In general, there are three types of professional wedding planners that you will encounter, but only two will be available for you to hire. The first is one who works for a company that specializes in wedding planning and often offers a range of services and products. The second works as an independent consultant who has a roster of vendors. (The advantage of hiring a third party like this is that she can head off touchy issues with vendors and members of your family.) Lastly, the third kind of wedding planner is one who works for the reception venue and whose job is to be the liaison between the venue and any vendors you may have on your team (including the wedding planner you've hired to work on your behalf), to make sure that all of the rules and restrictions related to the use of the venue are complied with, and that your venue is set up according to the agreement you signed when you made your deposit.

The Value of Good Advice

If the wedding planner you hired is a professional and does a good job, they can be an invaluable member of your support team. Their objectivity and professional experience can, in the long run, save you money by preventing you from making costly neophyte mistakes. For example, professional planners have extensive Rolodexes filled with vendors with whom they have longstanding relationships, and often these relationships can help you get discounts. It's customary for a planner to negotiate on your behalf for some or all of the services you will need for your wedding.

If you have decided to work with a planner, interview at least three people so that you can compare the candidates and see which ones meet your criteria. The following are some questions—some to ask the planner, and some to ask yourself:

- What was your first meeting like? Did you feel comfortable? Did you get a sense that this person could be relied on to keep things organized, on budget, and on time?

- Did the planner offer to give you references? If so, what did her clients say about their experience?

- Were you comfortable with the planner's management style and personality? Do you want someone who is a task master, or do you prefer someone more relaxed with a sense of humor?

- Did the planner listen to your concerns? Did he take notes?

- Did the meeting leave you feeling unsure about the planner's abilities or professional experience? Go with your gut instincts. If you have any doubts, move on. This is your day, and you have to feel comfortable with the person you select.

- What are the fees? Be specific about your budget, and make sure the wedding planner is comfortable with it and can work within it. (This would be the time to bring out your budget and worksheets so that the planner has a good idea of how much money you have allocated for each product and service you will need, how much time you have to plan, and what your goals are.)

- How does the planner's pricing structure work? Is it based on a flat fee or an hourly rate?

- Is a deposit required? If so, how much is due at the signing of the contract? Don't hire anyone without getting everything in writing.

Have a lawyer take a look at the agreement to make sure that you are protected if anything should go awry, and make sure that your contract clearly identifies any fees that may not be covered by the planner's agreement.

Photographer and/or Videographer

If you choose to work with a professional planner, and she has vendors she can recommend, be very clear with the planner about what you expect from the photographer and videographer and what shots you want to get. A good planner will negotiate with the photographers and videographers for the best price and service. If you choose to hire these people directly, be sure to negotiate a price that fits your budget. Always ask to see their portfolios, and get recommendations from other brides, your friends, and family. Be very clear about the look that you are going for, and if you don't like what you see, move on. If you aren't having any luck, a good source is the Professional Photographers of America at www.ppa.com, which has a large database of pros that you can search by location.

One thing to keep in mind as you search is that there are different types of photography and videography professionals—including those who work for studios, freelancers, and students—and they offer different levels of service.

Studio Photographer and/or Videographer

Many people think that studio photographers and videographers are more expensive, but the truth is that there is a service to match virtually any budget. It all depends on how much you are willing to pay and what kind of shots and images you are looking for. These kinds of pros can be more creative when taking your pictures (e.g., black-and-white photos and vintage-style photos). If you decide to hire someone who has their own studio, it may be less expensive since they won't have to add the cost of hiring a studio to your bill. As with any vendor, try to negotiate on price, and don't allow yourself to be pushed into paying for a service you either can't pay for

or don't feel fits your aesthetic. Also be aware that studio owners often have other photographers on staff. Make sure that you see and like the portfolio of the individual who will actually be shooting your wedding.

Freelance Photographer and/or Videographer

You can save some money by using a freelance photographer, who may be more flexible than a studio photographer because he doesn't have the same kinds of overhead that studios do. Keep in mind that even some studio photographers freelance on the side—you never know where you might find a freelance photographer. Check out sites like Craigslist.org, Guru.com, and Elance.com for freelancers, and remember to always get references. The best part about hiring a photographer is that nowadays, no matter which type of photographer you choose, you can see samples of their work online before you even decide to meet with someone.

Another benefit to using a freelancer is that at the end of the night, the freelancer may give you the rolls of film. Then you can have your wedding proofs developed at a discount drug store, choose the ones that you like, and then have the prints developed by a high-quality printer. Not all freelancers do this, however, so be sure to ask.

Student Photographer and/or Videographer

Another great option is to use a photography or videography/film student. You never know, you could have Ansel Adams or Steven Spielberg in your midst. There are several photography schools (see PhotographySchools .com for a directory) across the country that have listings of students who are for hire. Ask the school for a recommendation, or search for a student photographer on sites such as Craigslist.org. When meeting with the student, ask to view her work. Just as with any photographer, outline clear expectations, such as time of the event, hours needed, shots to be taken, etc.

Some Things You Should Avoid

In your zeal to save money and reduce costs, you may be inclined to cut corners on the cost of photography and videography, or you may be pressured by friends and family to use your photography-enthusiast cousin to take your pictures. Before you seriously consider this, remember that the pictures that you do or don't get that day will be the images that you will look at for years to come. Do you really want to risk having shots that are out of focus, that don't include the scenes you wanted to capture, or that include the backs of everyone's heads?

One option that can save some money and result in fun candid shots is to have disposable digital cameras at each table and let your guests play photographer. The pictures may not be professional quality, but they will have a genuine sentimentality to them that is priceless. There just isn't any substitute for heartfelt affection, and this often can be seen in the shots that your friends and family get throughout the festivities.

The advent of disposable digital cameras has made it possible to cut down on the cost of developing pictures, because you can use online photo editing and photo galleries to manipulate and save on the images you like the most. Some of the best online products to help you edit your images, put them into albums (complete with music and scrapbooking tools), and share them with others include SmileBox.com, Flickr.com, Picknik.com, and PhotoScape.com. If you insist on printing out your photos, places like Costco and Sam's Club can develop your prints as well as save the images on a CD that you can edit later.

How to Keep Your Cool

Aside from sticking to your budget, having a good support team, being organized, and involving the groom in the planning, here are some tips for how to reduce stress as you tick off the days, weeks, and months before your wedding day arrives:

- Remember the big picture. A wedding is meant to be a happy time, so keep in mind that you are gathering together your friends and family to celebrate the union of two families.

- Never underestimate the importance of good communication. Every step along the way, you want to keep people informed and up-to-date. This includes communication between you and the groom, between each of you and your parents, between you and your friends, and with the wedding attendants, vendors, and the rest of your support team.

- Remember who you are and what your values are. Don't lose your identity in a rush to please everyone.

- Continue to do the things that have meaning for you. If that means taking your weekly yoga class, then do it. Don't lose touch with your friends, who can be an invaluable lifeline and source of moral support.

- Make time for you and the groom to do things together that deepen your commitment to each other. You could take dancing lessons together so that your first dance isn't awkward for either one of you.

- Lean on the members of your support team and give them the tasks that you don't mind delegating. If you aren't that interested in tracking down the music or entertainment for the reception but your sister wants to be responsible for that task, then by all means, let her do it.

- Get ideas from other brides about how they weathered the stresses of wedding planning. Check out blogs like DCNearlyWeds.com or online forums like WeddingsOnline.ie to get advice and tips from thousands of other brides.

- For your sake and the sake of your future life together with your new husband, take the time to appreciate why you fell in love with other in the first place. Relish this special time together and savor every moment.

If you do these things, then you will have happy memories to look back on later. Most importantly, you can rest assured that you have done your best to have a tax-deductible wedding that saved you money.

After the Wedding

Congratulations! You did it! You made it down the aisle in one piece. Now that you're married, what's next? You've saved a boatload of money thanks to the valuable tips and tricks in this book, so you'll need to figure out what to do with that. And then, of course, there's just getting used to being married and adjusting to your new life together with your groom.

What to Do with the Money You Have Saved

You may be thinking a cute outfit (with shoes to match), but—hear me out before you throw your old shoes at me—you should invest the money you've saved instead. You're probably rolling your eyes and thinking, "What

do I know about investing? I wouldn't know what to invest in anyway. It would be so much easier to just put it toward bills." That's not true, because you have already learned the basics of managing a budget. Why not invest in your future instead of spending your future now? Investing is still important even though the market has been up and down. It is a valuable tool you can use to help secure your financial future. Decide which products work for you (such as CDs, stocks, mutual funds, and so on) and, as always, consult your groom, your tax advisor, and/or your financial planner concerning your situation. The money you saved using the tips in this book could help you secure a down payment for that house you have wanted to buy. If you are still in the throes of fixing your credit, give it time, and maybe continue renting. Which is the better choice for you?

The Pros and Cons of Renting vs. Buying

There are many benefits to buying versus renting, not the least of which are building wealth and equity. In addition, you can also write off the first ten years or so of interest payments, which helps lower your tax burden. As a homeowner, you are free to change the interior as you wish and make it your own. Compared to renting, however, owning a home can be a financial burden, including upkeep, property taxes, and other costs that renters don't have to pay.

When you rent, you have the flexibility and freedom to move on short notice; you don't have maintenance costs, because the landlord takes care of repairs; and depending on the markets' ups and downs, renting may be cheaper than buying. Plus, if you save money, you can use it to pay off debts to buy a house. What you don't get with renting is the tax deduction of the interest on your mortgage, you lose out entirely on the wealth-building power of owning a home, and you are living in someone else's property.

Securing a Down Payment

If you have not already started thinking about this, you may want to use the extra money you saved on your wedding toward a down payment for a house. There are several programs that can help first-time homebuyers, and depending on income, the qualifying amount can change. One such program is the America Dream Down Payment Act, which was instituted in 2003 to provide homebuyers with assistance for closing costs and down payments. Several of these programs have income restrictions, so be sure to read all the fine print. In addition, there are several programs nationwide that offer varying interest rates, including grants that provide lower interest rates, as well as assistance with down payments, closing costs, and housing counseling.

Happily Ever After

By now you have probably built up expectations and fantasies about married life, and your first year will be one of adjustment. You may have thought you knew your hubby, but it is not until you live with someone day to day that you truly get to know their habits. I want to send you off with some words of encouragement, because after all of the hoopla of the wedding planning, the ceremony, the reception, the honeymoon, the sending of thank you cards, etc., you may feel like coming back home is slightly anticlimactic. You have spent probably close to a year living and breathing your wedding plans, and now you must come back and make the big transition to married life. If you are feeling a little blue, don't be alarmed. This is more common than you think, and many brides feel this way. It's a little like the way new mothers feel when they come home with a new baby and realize what a big step being a mother really is and how it will change their life forever. Don't panic, because there are some things that you can do to help you cope.

Surviving the Postwedding Blues

After all of the photos have come back and you can finally put all of your pictures in frames, you can now relish the memories from your wedding. Take the time to relive the happy moments with your new husband and revel in your new relationship as husband and wife. Once you go back to work and begin living a normal life, you may find that you are still on an emotional roller coaster. The following are some simple things that you can do to keep the blues away:

- Communicate with your husband about your feelings. Now that you are living together as husband and wife, you may find that there is some tension between you as you get used to each other's habits. Be open and accepting of your husband's quirks and share how you feel about the postwedding letdown and your new life. This will help prevent major conflicts or underlying tensions from spoiling your special time as newlyweds. Each of you will make mistakes; that is only natural.

- Overlook the little things, and learn how to pick your battles. It isn't worth having a big blowout over small things. Resolve to forgive and forget.

- Seek the advice of someone you trust. If you feel like you need some guidance on how to cope, don't feel guilty or embarrassed. Sometimes an objective third party can lend a helpful ear and give you some needed perspective. Make sure that the person you confide in is discreet so that your revelations don't get spread around or repeated to your husband, which could cause unnecessary heartache.

In the end, all that matters is that you remember the reason you went through this process in the first place: because you wanted to share your lives together. No, it is not easy, but I hope you learned some helpful tips along the way so that at least you don't have to worry about getting yourself out of a huge amount of debt because you overspent. If you planned properly, saved as much money as you could, and developed a solid financial plan together, you can only grow stronger as a happy couple and truly live happily ever after.

Resources

Chapter 1: The Cost of Today's Weddings

Bridal Shows

Bridal Club: www.bridesclub.com

The Great Bridal Expo: www.greatbridalexpo.com

One Wed: www.onewed.com

Online Bridal Shows: www.onlinebridalshows.com

Washington Bridal Showcase: www.bridalshowcase.com

Wed Alert: www.wedalert.com

Wedding Basics: www.weddingbasics.com

Wedding Wire: www.weddingwire.com/wedding-events

Chapter 2: Getting Organized and Managing Your Wedding

General Wedding Advice

BridesandGrooms.com

PashWeddings.com

TheKnot.com

WeddingSolutions.com

Portals and Directories

Bridal Network: www.bridalnetwork.ca

The Flirty Guide: www.flirtyguide.com

Wedding Planning

Miss Now Mrs: www.missnowmrs.com (changing your name made simple online)

Top Table Planner: www.toptableplanner.com (seat-planning software)

The Wedding-Planning Community
BrideandGroom Planner.com
EZWeddingPlanner.com

Wedding Styles/Traditions
DestinationWeddings.com
ForBlackWeddings.com
InStyleWeddings.com
IslandBrides.com (for destination weddings in the Caribbean)
OffbeatBride.com

Chapter 3: For Love or Money

Credit
Annual Credit Report: www.annualcreditreport.com
Equifax: www.equifax.com
Experian: www.experian.com
TransUnion: www.transunion.com

Financial Planning
Bank Rate: www.bankrate.com (financial calculators and tools)
Cost Helper: www.costhelper.com
Cost of Wedding: www.costofwedding.com
DreamBuilder savings account from Mercantile Bank:
    www.mercantilebk.com/personal/bc/dreambuilder-choice.php
IRS: www.irs.gov
Num Sum: www.numsum.com (track your wedding budget)
QuickBooks: http://quickbooks.intuit.com
Quicken: http://quicken.intuit.com

Chapter 4: The Tax-Deductible Wedding

Charities

Assisted Living: www.assistedlivinginfo.com

Brides Against Breast Cancer: www.bridesagainstbreastcancer.org

Feeding America (formerly America's Second Harvest):
   www.feedingamerica.org

Goodwill: www.goodwill.org

I Do Foundation: www.idofoundationorg

Just Give: www.justgive.org

National Coalition Against Domestic Violence: www.ncadv.org

Nursing Homes Nationwide: www.nursinghomeinfo.com

Ronald McDonald House Charities: www.rmhc.org

Salvation Army: www.salvationarmyusa.org

Honeymoon Registries

The Big Day: www.thebigday.com

Disney's Honeymoon Registry: www.honeymoonregistry.disney
   .go.com

Honey Luna, the Honeymoon Registry Service: wwwhoneyluna.com

Honeymoon Wishes: www.honeymoonwishes.com

Traveler's Joy: www.travelersjoy.com

National Parks/Botanical Gardens

American Public Gardens Association: www.publicgardens.org

GORP: www.gorp.com

The National Park Service: www.nps.gov

Preowned Bridal Gowns

Bridal Garden: www.bridalgarden.org

Brides Against Breast Cancer: www.bridesagainstbreastcancer.org

Encore Bridal: www.encorebridal.com

Preowned Wedding Dresses: www.preownedweddingdresses.com

Wore It Once: www.woreitonce.com (connects buyers and sellers of used wedding gowns, bridesmaids' dresses, and other special-occasion dresses)

Volunteering
Global Cross Road: www.globalcrossroad.com
Global Vision International (GVI): www.gvi.co.uk
Global Volunteer Network (GVN): www.volunteer.org.nz
Global Volunteers: www.globalvolunteers.org
Habitat for Humanity: www.habitat.org
Idealist: www.idealist.org
U.S. Department of State: www.state.gov
World Volunteer Web: www.worldvolunteerweb.org

Chapter 5: Savings You Never Knew Existed

DIY
Do It Yourself: www.doityourself.com
Joann Fabric and Crafts: www.joann.com
Michaels, the Arts & Crafts Store: www.michaels.com

House Sitters/House Swapping
Home Exchange: www.homeexchange.com
HouseCarers: www.housecarers.com
House Sitting America: www.housesitteramerica.com
Intervac: www.intervac.com

Wedding Cake Rental
Cake Rental: www.cakerental.com
Rent the Cake of Your Dreams: www.rentthecakeofyourdreams.com

Chapter 6: The Beauty of Sponsorship and Bartering

Bartering

    Barter Planet: www.barterplanet.com
    Barter Your Service: www.barteryourservice.com
    Craigslist: www.craiglist.org
    People Trading Services: www.peopletradingservices.com

Chapter 7: The Ecotechno Wedding

Biodegradable Confetti

    Beau-Coup: www.beau-coup.com
    Ecoparti: www.ecoparti.com
    Flutter Fetti: www.flutterfetti.com

Conflict-Free Jewelry

    Brilliant Earth: www.brilliantearth.com
    Dawes Design: http://dawes-design.com (offers recycled gold and conflict-free diamonds)
    Green Karat: www.greenkarat.com
    Leber Jeweler: www.leberjeweler.com

Ecofriendly Clothing, Housewares, and Gifts

    Boll Organic: www.bollorganic.com (men's organic shirts)
    Downbound: www.downbound.com (housewares and clothing)
    Eco Express Gifts: www.ecoexpress.com
    EcoWise: www.ecowise.com (offers clothes and housewares)
    Grass Root Natural Goods: www.grassrootsnaturalgoods.com (offers natural household goods and clothing)
    GreenCulture House Wares: www.ecohousewares.com
    Green Feet: www.greenfeet.com

A Natural Home: www.anaturalhome.com
Terra Pass: www.terrapass.com
3r Living: www.3rliving.com
Viva Terra: www.vivaterra.com

Ecofriendly Wedding Apparel

Flair Bridesmaid: www.flairbridesmaid.com

Get Conscious: www.getconscious.com (their fabrics are made from all hemp blends, and they also sell men's hemp suits, flowergirl dresses, and other eco-conscious apparel)

Great Green Wedding: www.greatgreenwedding.com (offers an array of women and men's clothing, accessories, footwear, and sleepwear)

Wedding apparel: www.greeneleganceweddings.com

Ecofriendly Wedding Invitations and Favors

Botanical PaperWorks: www.botanicalpaperworks.com (favors and invitations)

Earthly Affair: www.earthlyaffair.com

Greenfield Paper: www.greenfieldpaper.com

Theo Chocolate: www.theochocolate.com (offers organic chocolate favors)

Twisted Limb Paper: www.twistedlimbpaper.com (specializes in handmade 100 percent recycled paper products)

Floral Wholesalers

Fifty Flowers: www.fiftyflowers.com

Growers Box: www.growersbox.com

Potomac Floral Wholesale: www.flowerwholesale.com

Green Honeymoons/Sustainable Travel

Green Globe: www.ec3globsl.com

Green Hotels/Green Hotel Association: www.greenhotels.com

Green Visions: www.greenvisions.ba
Eco Tourism: www.ecotourism.org
EcoTrotters: www.ecotrotters.com
Sierra Club: www.sierraclub.org
Sustainable Travel: www.sustainabletravel.com

Organic Spirits

Appellation NYC: www.appellationnyc.com
Diamond Organics: www.diamondorganics.com (sells organic
    champagne and sparkling wine)
Organic Champagne: www.organic-champagne.com (a UK-based site
    that sells organic champagne, wine, and mixers)
The Organic Wine Company: www.theorganicwinecompany.com
Organic Wine Journal: www.organicwinejournal.com

Organic, Vegetarian, and Vegan Caterers

California

Om Organics: www.omorganics.org
Seedling Organic Catering: www.seedlingcatering.com
Vegetarian Weddings: www.vegetarianweddings.com

Colorado

Eco Goddess: http://eco-goddess.com

District of Columbia

Gail's Vegetarian: www.gailsvegetarian.com

Massachusetts

Catering by Dinner Is Served: www.veggiecatering.com

Minnesota

Pharm Catering: www.pharmcatering.com

New York

Lucid Food: www.lucidfood.com

Two Brothers Catering: www.twobrotherscatering.com

North Carolina

Bearfoot Catering: www.bearfootcatering.com

Washington State

Herban Feast: www.herbanfeast.com

Macrina Bakery: www.macrinabakery.com

Ravishing Radish: www.ravishingradish.com

Organic Wedding Flowers

California Certified Organic Farmers (CCOF): www.ccof.org

California Organic Flowers: www.californiaorganicflowers.com

Diamond Organics: www.diamondorganics.com

Flower by the Sea: www.fbts.com

Lavender Farm: www.lavenderfarm.com

Organic Bouquet: www.organicbouquet.com (they donate a portion of the proceeds to a charitable foundation)

Organic-Wine Blogs

Eco Wine: www.ecowine.com

Organic Vintners: www.organicvintners.com

Photos/Online Photo Sharing

Flickr: www.flickr.com

Fotki: www.fotki.com

Photo Works: www.photoworks.com

Shutterfly: www.shutterfly.com

Smugmug: www.smugmug.com

Snapfish: www.snapfish.com

You Shoot: www.youshoot.com

Planning the Green Wedding

Eco-Chic Weddings: www.ecochicweddings.com

Green Elegance Weddings: www.greeneleganceweddings.com

Portovert: www.portovert.com (a general green wedding site self-described as "The Gateway to Greener Weddings")

Social Networking/Blog Sites

Bride.com: www.bride.com

Brides.com: www.brides.com

The Brides Cafe: www.thebridescafe.com

Eco Chic Weddings: www.ecochicweddings.typepad.com

Facebook: www.facebook.com

The Knot: www.theknot.com

Lazy Bride: www.lazybride.com

MySpace: www.myspace.com

Polk A Dot Bride: www.polkadotbride.com/wp

The Preppy Wedding: www.thepreppywedding.blogspot.com

Style Me Pretty: www.stylemepretty.com

Wedding Bee: www.weddingbee.com

WeddingWire: www.weddingwire.com

Blogs for the Groom

Groom Groove Blog: www.groomgrove.com

Grooms Advice: www.groomsadvice.com

Start Your Own Blog

Blogger: www.blogger.com

Six Apart: www.sixapart.com

Word Press: http://wordpress.org

Sustainable Fabrics

Conscious Clothing: www.getconscious.com

Denver Fabrics: www.denverfabrics.com

Green Sage: www.greensage.com
Near Sea Naturals: www.nearseanaturals.com
Sweetgrass Natural Fibers: www.sweetgrassfibers.com

Chapter 8: Your Core Support Team

For the Groom and Groomsmen
Advice

GroomsAdvice.com
Groom411.com
GroomGroove.com
GroomsOnline.com
TheManRegistry.com

Wedding Attire

After Hours Formalwear: www.afterhours.com
International Formal Association: www.formalwear.org
Island Importers: www.islandimporter.com (beach wedding attire for
    men and women)
Men's Warehouse: www.menswearhouse.com
MyOwnTuxedo: www.myowntuxedo.com (preowned tuxedos)
Tuxedo Junction: www.tuxedojunction.com
Tuxedos Online: www.tuxedosonline.com (a tuxedo superstore)
Tuxedo Wholesaler: www.tuxedowholesaler.com (sells tuxedos and
    retro suits)

Wedding Consultants

Association of Bridal Consultants: www.bridalassn.com

Index

Acknowledgments

I would like to thank the wonderful folks at Globe Pequot Press, *especially* Heather Carreiro, *for believing in this project and providing support and guidance.*

To Diane Nine, my agent: I could not have gotten through this process without you providing the foundation. Your honesty, humor, and direction kept me on the right path. Thank you for making this dream possible.

To Summer Whitford, Book Doctor: You knew a chance meeting during jury duty would lead to a book. I think there are no chance meetings, and we happened to be in the right place at the right time. Thank you for your help and insight. My appreciation for your help is beyond measure.

To Dad and my maternal and paternal families (the Britts, the Hardys, and the Rivers): Because of who you are, I am who I am. Thanks for your continued love and support. I'm living proof that it takes a village to raise a child, and I have an amazing village.

To my friends, the day-to-day crew: Thanks for being a wonderful support system throughout the birthdays, bad hair days, job losses, flat tires, promotions, and the happy moments—I am looking forward to growing older with all of you.

About the Author

After attending a plethora of weddings, and hearing about the cost before and after, Sabrina Rivers thought there must be a better way. This book is a result of her curiosity and the need to answer the questions: Why does a wedding cost so much? And how can it be more affordable?

Sabrina Rivers is a marketing and health care professional. She resides in Maryland.